The publication of *Ship, Sea and Sky: The Marine Art of James Edward Buttersworth* was made possible by a generous grant from The Henry Luce Foundation, Inc.

First published in 1994 in the United States of America by
Rizzoli International Publications, Inc.
300 Park Avenue South
New York, New York 10010

Library of Congress Cataloging-in-Publication Data
Grassby, Richard B.
    Ship, sea & sky : the marine art of James Edward Buttersworth / by
Richard B. Grassby ; foreword by Peter Neill.
        p.   cm.
    "Published in association with the South Street Seaport Museum."
    Includes bibliographical references.
    ISBN 0-8478-1805-5
    1. Buttersworth, James Edward, 1817–1894—Criticism and interpre-
tation. 2. Ships in art. 3. Sea in art. I. Title. II. Title: Ship, sea and sky.
    ND237.B98G73   1994
    759.13—dc20   93-42623
                                                       CIP

Designed by Lawrence Wolfson
Printed in Singapore
Jacket: see plate 31

Page 1. NEW YORK YACHT CLUB RACE, *20¼ × 30¼", Mystic Seaport Museum, Inc., Mystic, Connecticut, Photograph by Mary Anne Stets*

Here Buttersworth adopted a deep open foreground and concentrated the action in the middle ground. Although the American man-of-war and the two steamers carrying spectators open the low horizon, they tend to crowd the canvas with relevant but distracting detail. Buttersworth sometimes juxtaposed unrelated objects or partially intercepted and subdued an object. As in plate 26, the competitors are rounding a buoy at different angles, but here the dramatic impact is reinforced by foreshortening and by the direction of the leading yachts, which approach the viewer bow forward.

Page 4. THE CLIPPER "WITCHCRAFT," *27 × 35", Private collection, Photo courtesy of collector*

Built by Paul Curtis of Chelsea for William D. Pickman and Richard S. Rogers of Salem, the *Witchcraft* (187' × 39' × 22'; 1,310 tons) had a witch on a broomstick for a figurehead and was eventually lost near Hatteras on April 8, 1861. Buttersworth pays homage here to the craftsmanship and speed of this famous clipper, which he depicted with a salty veracity and blunt, nautical detail. The low lines and filled sails suggest great momentum through the water under strong winds; the secondary vessel on the horizon may be a starboard view of the same ship.

Richard B. Grassby

SHIP, SEA & SKY

THE MARINE ART OF JAMES EDWARD BUTTERSWORTH

SOUTH STREET SEAPORT MUSEUM
IN ASSOCIATION WITH

TABLE OF CONTENTS

6
ACKNOWLEDGMENTS
Richard B. Grassby

7
FOREWORD
Peter Neill

9
INTRODUCTION

PLATES
Early Paintings 58
Clippers and Packet Ships 64
Steamships and Steamboats 71
Storm Scenes 76
Mastering the Elements 83
Yachting in New York Harbor 88
America's Cup Trials and Races 96
Famous Yachts in Action 101
Yachts and Other Sailing Craft 106
Portscapes and Seascapes 114

121
NOTES

126
SUGGESTIONS FOR FURTHER READING

ACKNOWLEDGMENTS

This exhibition celebrates the talent and subject matter of marine painter James Edward Buttersworth as well as American maritime history and art. His importance as an American marine artist was recognized as early as 1939, when the Metropolitan Museum of Art in New York included *Magic off Sandy Hook* in its exhibition *Life in America*, and the same painting was shown by the Museum of Fine Arts Boston in 1943. The only previous exhibition devoted entirely to Buttersworth was mounted by Mystic Seaport Museum in 1975. Since many of his important paintings are dispersed among private collections, the examples presented here have been chosen to demonstrate the quality and range of his work, so that we can now view and appreciate his art as a coherent whole.

A great debt is owed to Rudolph Schaefer's *J. E. Buttersworth*, published in 1975 with extensive illustrations and astute comments; Mrs. Janet Schaefer generously made available the photographs and documentation on which that work was based. Mr. Glen Foster also carefully reviewed the text and offered valuable suggestions at every stage of planning. This exhibition could not have been assembled and mounted without the unstinting help of private collectors, private and public corporations, museums, and dealers, all of whom offered valuable information and advice, and many of whom loaned items from their collections. The following individuals and institutions should be acknowledged: Vose Galleries, the Old Print Shop, Brian Oliphant, Christie's, Hirschl & Adler Galleries, Mystic Seaport Museum, Mariners' Museum, Maine Maritime Museum, the Museum of the City of New York, the Peabody Essex Museum, the Penobscot Museum, the New York Yacht Club, Levy, Inc., and Smith Gallery.

I am grateful to the South Street Seaport Museum for allowing me this opportunity to address Buttersworth and the place of marine art in the greater context of the fine arts. Specifically, I am indebted to the trustees, most especially Fritz Gold, and to the staff—Peter Neill, Paula Mayo, Cathi Comar Quintana, Daniel Beaudoin, and Paul Pearson—who have given so generously of their time to supplement and to support these efforts. In addition, I would like to thank Dan Monroe, Director, and Dan Finamore, Acting Curator of Maritime History, of the Peabody Essex Museum; and Robert Donnelley, Director, and Scott Atkinson, Curator of Collections and Exhibitions, of the Terra Museum of American Art for their contributions to this project.

Finally, I would like to thank Charles Miers, Jennifer Condon, and Elizabeth White at Rizzoli, and designer Lawrence Wolfson, for bringing this book to fruition.

RICHARD B. GRASSBY

F O R E W O R D

When art historian Richard Grassby and I first discussed the idea of a traveling exhibition of marine painting, we quickly agreed that James Edward Buttersworth, above all his contemporaries, deserved far more serious consideration as an artist exemplary of the primary themes of nineteenth-century America: the impetus for discovery, technological innovation, belief in progress, and reverence for Nature. Thus Buttersworth's art could—and should—be appreciated alongside that of the Hudson River School, for example, or of the painters of Cape Ann or western expansion, and would not be found wanting either in content or technique.

The exhibit demonstrates how easily Buttersworth transcended the conventions of traditional ship portraiture, the mechanical aspect of much "pierhead" painting that is so frequently pointed to by critics desiring to belittle marine art as a serious genre. He was quite evidently a more accomplished artist than his maritime competitors and, despite the vocational necessities of his trade, consistently produced more pleasing, complex, and evocative paintings than the other artists of his place and time.

The examples included here, then, have been chosen to make this argument. These yachting scenes and images of ships in extremis share his best artistic qualities: authentic detail, elegant composition, sophisticated color, refined qualities of light, and a palpable dynamism that is absent from the work of artistic equals who nonetheless chose

to depict immobile subjects in static landscapes. Moreover, this technical accomplishment is focused on the image of the ship, set in an ever-changing environment of sea and sky, resulting arguably in a catalog of successful metaphor for the themes mentioned above. The ship *was* the primary vessel of nineteenth-century discovery; the ship, driven by sail, then steam, *was* the highest evolution of contemporary technology; the ship *was* the viable agent for progress as measured by world immigration and trade; the ship *was* a transcendent symbol of adaptation to the extraordinary forces of Nature and Change. To all this, I submit that James Edward Buttersworth may legitimately lay claim.

PETER NEILL
President
South Street Seaport Museum

The exhibition "Ship, Sea and Sky: The Marine Art of James Edward Buttersworth" has been made possible through grants from the National Endowment for the Arts, the New York State Council for the Arts, L. Scott Frantz, Glen Foster, and Fritz Gold. Publication of this catalogue is the result of a generous subvention by the Henry Luce Foundation, whose support for such catalogues has made an incomparable contribution to art historical scholarship. The South Street Seaport Museum is grateful.

THE S.S. "CHICKAMAUGA"
20 × 26"
Unsigned
Courtesy The Mariners' Museum, Newport News, Virginia

This British-built twin-screw blockade-runner and raider was originally named the *Edith*. She was purchased by the Confederate navy in 1864 and commissioned under Capt. J. Nicholson. Lightly armed with a spar-deck battery of three rifled guns, she captured several prizes off New York, but was scuttled when Wilmington was evacuated. The indirect lighting, dark foreground, bank of frothy clouds behind the ship, and pink striations in the sky are characteristic effects (see plate 12).

INTRODUCTION

THE HISTORICAL CONTEXT

To understand the work of James Edward Buttersworth requires some acquaintance with the world he inhabited, since it stimulated his artistic sensibility. During his long life, technological, political, and economic changes transformed the United States into a rich and powerful nation and made New York City the country's leading distributive, financial, and cultural center. This historical background can be reconstructed with relative ease, but details of Buttersworth's life and personal relationships are sparse. No correspondence or family papers have survived, and Buttersworth may not have been fully literate; his wife and stepmother, for example, marked the birth documents of their children with an X.[1] He was remembered by his descendants as a kindly and humorous man who took cold baths and long walks every morning, observed the English tea ritual, loved cats and music, and was a poor businessman.[2] Further aspects of his character and interests must be inferred from his paintings.

Buttersworth was one of many early American artists who were either emigrants from England or of English parentage.[3] He was descended from an artisan family with branches both in the Isle of Wight and London. His marriage certificate states that his father was Thomas, a marine painter. What evidence there is, however, suggests that there were two marine painters named Thomas Buttersworth.[4] The elder of the two was born in the Isle of Wight and was baptized on May 6, 1768; his birth date also can be ascertained from the age he gave in 1795, when he enlisted in the Royal Navy. He began to paint while in the service and became a professional marine artist after his discharge in 1800. The exhibition records of the Royal Academy reveal that by 1813 he resided at 15 Golden Lane, Kensington in Surrey, and in the 1820s he lived at Trafalgar Street, Walworth in Surrey. Although the date of his death cannot be established unequivocally, it is likely that he died in 1828.[5]

The younger Thomas lived at Callarns, Little Marlborough, and Little Hamblyn streets in Greenwich. He died on November 25, 1842, and was buried in St. Alfrege Church, Greenwich; since his death certificate clearly records an age of forty-five, he would have been born in 1797.[6] The elder Thomas could have had two sons, Thomas and James, but it is unlikely that he sired James at the age of fifty and more likely that he was James's grandfather. The younger Thomas married his first wife in 1816 and subsequently married Gertrude Maestres and had children by her in 1838 and 1841, including a son named Thomas. But it was his first wife who produced James, in January 1817. Although no baptismal record has been found, when James died on March 2, 1894, the death certificate stated that he was seventy-seven years two months.[7] It is true that his age was given as thirty-one in the 1850 census, but there are discrepancies in the return between the known and stated ages of his children, and his death certificate is more likely to be accurate.[8]

Like many English artists, James Buttersworth was brought up in a family that practiced marine painting as a hereditary craft, and he probably began working at the trade in his late teens. On October 11, 1838, when he was twenty-one, he married Ann Plowman, two months after the birth of their daughter. They lived on the outer fringe of London, close to the Thames, at Bethnal Green, Greenwich, and Lambeth. The London Directory of 1845 lists his address as Howland Street, Fitzroy Square. Sometime between the birth of his fourth child, in July 1845, and 1848 he decided to emigrate to America, where his fifth and last child was born. Although he cannot be identified on any passenger list, it is likely that he traveled to New York in 1847.[9] His wife and children probably came later. He was certainly in Manhattan by 1848, since he was listed at

345 Greenwich Street in a city directory of 1849–1850.[10]

His motives for coming to America can only be presumed, but he probably felt that he could improve his financial position. Like most English marine artists, Buttersworth was a self-employed artisan of modest means. His wife was the daughter of a laborer, and the houses he rented were typical of those built for the working class. By 1847 Buttersworth's father was probably dead, and although James may have acquired some capital through inheritance, his family was growing and the English economy was in recession. The majority of immigrants to New York during the Hungry Forties were German and Irish, but the outflow from England also reached a peak.[11] A handbook for British immigrants in 1840 claimed that there were opportunities in New York for house and ship painters, although a few well-established native artists were said to monopolize commissions in the limited market for portraits, landscapes, and figure subjects, and there was a surplus of engravers.[12]

Buttersworth spent the remainder of his life in the vicinity of New York City. He died in West Hoboken on March 2, 1894, and is buried at Grove Church cemetery in North Bergen, New Jersey. He may have visited England around 1851 for the Cowes regatta, since several paintings of the *America's* victory that year suggest firsthand knowledge, and a set of drawings of English yachts is dated 1851.[13] The settings of his paintings range from Boston to South America, but there is no hard evidence that he ever visited other ports. Although a painting by Buttersworth of a rescue at sea is known to have been bought from an address in Brooklyn, his residence in New York City was brief. In the city, artists usually had to rent airless attic rooms above commercial establishments or boardinghouses, whereas in rural New Jersey Buttersworth could afford a house. Here, among marshes and meadows, sportsmen still hunted in the landscapes that served as models for Asher Brown Durand and Martin Johnson Heade.[14] West Hoboken, which was not incorporated until 1880 and was later renamed Union City, was a mere village, but its common was large enough to serve as a Union camp during the Civil War.[15]

On October 29, 1849, Buttersworth paid $450 for several plots of land and a small house described as a "Swiss cottage" in West Hoboken, listed merely as 247 Paterson Avenue in the 1850 census, but which later became number 447.[16] He was still living in that house at the time of the 1888 census. Ann Buttersworth also owned property in her own right. In 1849 and 1869 she bought several plots of land, and

at her death on December 23, 1886, she had $400 in cash and $5,000 in real estate, including two houses on Paterson Avenue, which she bequeathed to her children with a life interest for her husband.[17] Buttersworth lived alone for a few years, but eventually moved in with his eldest son, also called James, who lived nearby at 728 Paterson Avenue and probably had a studio on the third floor.[18] His widowed daughter, Ann Graff, lived at Pleasant Plaine, Staten Island.[19] The administrators of Buttersworth's estate could not trace his other surviving son, Charles, who had not been heard of for two years.[20] Although Buttersworth did not enjoy the wealthy life-style of marine artist Fred Pansing, his estate at death amounted to a respectable $1,650.38, most of which, judging by the dividend income, was probably deposited in a savings account.[21]

Buttersworth lived through more than four decades during which American shipping underwent continuous and momentous change. New York was then primarily a maritime city, and it overtook the New England and southern ports to become the nation's leading transportation center. In 1840, 414,000 tons, or one-fifth of all U.S. tonnage, were registered in New York, which was second only to London; the number of vessels doubled and included between 500 and 700 sailing craft and fifty steamships. Between 1865 and 1870 the number of coastal vessels arriving and departing rose from 14,370 to 28,665.[22] The enormous volume and congestion of shipping is well conveyed by contemporary watercolors and prints.[23] In addition to the hundreds of inland, coastal, and oceangoing vessels loading and discharging and maneuvering in the rivers and bays, scores of ferries plied between Manhattan, Brooklyn, New Jersey, and Long Island. The names of ships, their cargoes, and passage times were common knowledge.[24]

It is difficult now to appreciate the importance of transportation by water before the development of bridges and road transport. The ship was as ubiquitous as the modern automobile and came in every shape and size. By 1847 South Street had become the nerve center of maritime commerce, and the masts of the great square-riggers at the piers towered over the buildings. But they were still greatly outnumbered by the lesser brigs, brigantines, and barques and by a host of small fore- and aft-rigged sloops and schooners, barges, cutters, and pilot boats. Even before the transatlantic steamer became a familiar sight, there was no shortage of steam riverboats, ferries, and tugboats. New York therefore provided James Buttersworth with an inexhaustible source

of raw material and inspiration. When he crowded his harbor views of New York with vessels, he was accurately reflecting reality.

Buttersworth was in a position to witness the heyday of the packet and clipper. In the early nineteenth century, New York merchants and shipowners dominated the Atlantic trade by introducing scheduled services; the new packets, unlike the old regular traders, hauled freight and passengers in all weather.[25] Although Boston followed suit, the Black Ball, the Red Star, and other packet lines made the Liverpool–New York route the main highway between Europe and America. Regional staples, in particular Southern cotton, provided eastward freight to balance the westward flow of European immigrants and manufactures; two-thirds of the 5.4 million immigrants between 1819 and 1866 landed at New York. The packets doubled in size to around one thousand tons by 1842, and although overshadowed after 1848 by the clippers, they performed better against the prevailing winds in the Atlantic. Ships like the *Dreadnought* (plate 7) were strong, dry, and comfortable as well as fast, and they brought over most of the immigrants until 1865. They provided the backbone of merchant sail and competed for world trade with the vessels of other maritime nations.

A SQUARE-RIGGER OFF THE ISLE OF SHOALS
20 × 30"
Private collection
Photograph by Lynton Gardiner

In this naturalistic study of a square-rigger maneuvering in a realistic sea, there are traces of Dutch influence, probably filtered through English models. Like the Dutch masters, Buttersworth could portray a sense of the continuity of the sea and the interaction of light and water; he also employed a delicately modulated gray wash for atmospheric effect and favored a lively sea and banks of clouds.

The discovery of gold in California and the initial demand for transport and supplies that followed also expanded business with the Pacific coast, via both Cape Horn and the combined land-and-sea route through Panama.

In response to economic opportunities, ships became faster. American vessels, which so often had to function as smugglers, privateers, slavers, and blockade-runners, had always been designed for speed. The ability to outrun pirates and more heavily armed adversaries and to transport tea and spices from China quickly enough to maintain their freshness relied on swift vessels. New records were continuously set by the clippers, whose speeds could no longer be accurately measured by the old log line. In 1849 the *Sea Witch* reached Hong Kong from New York in seventy-four days, fourteen hours; the *Sovereign of the Seas* reached Honolulu from New York in eighty-two days and Liverpool in thirteen days, twenty-two hours.[26] Since speed was in part a function of size, each new clipper was larger than its predecessor; the masts of the *Sovereign of the Seas* were a yard thick.

The classic clipper, a description that applies strictly to a particular hull design, appeared in the 1840s, but it evolved in stages over time. It was preceded by the Baltimore clipper, which itself had developed from the long, low,

flush-decked schooners and brigs of the Chesapeake, which in turn had been influenced by French designs (plate 6). The long, curving bow was adopted in 1841 by John W. Griffith, a marine architect of New York, and in 1843 his concept was first tried in the *Rainbow* and then in the *Howqua* and *Sea Witch*.[27] In Boston, the talented designer Donald McKay built a whole string of famous clippers, including *Flying Cloud* (plate 17), the *Sovereign of the Seas*, and the ill-fated *Great Republic* (plate 9).[28] In the past, tonnage duty rules had encouraged architects to design abnormally deep ships with a uniform beam. The clipper, by contrast, had a sharp entry to cut through water with breadth of beam and a low center of gravity. Its long hull was V-shaped at the ends, rather than U-shaped, and its greater depth of hold improved stability and prevented leeway.[29] It was stronger, more buoyant, and easier to handle and maneuver.

Some clippers, such as the *Architect* or William Webb's *Young America*, were built as much for durability and for cargo capacity in relation to tonnage as for speed (plates 6 and 16).[30] But shipowners—inspired by dramatic runs and initial profits—overbuilt and swamped the market. Although magnificent specimens of nautical design and breathtaking under full sail, the later and more extreme clippers proved uneconomic. Because they cut through the sea without lift, they were extremely wet ships and difficult to maintain.[31] Driven extremely hard, they were frequently dismasted or lost their spars. Unlike the whalers, whose timbers were preserved by sperm oil, the extreme clippers had short working lives.[32] Their cargo and passenger capacity was halved by their design, and they required large crews: The *Sovereign of the Seas* had a complement of 105. Consequently, they needed to command high rates of carriage on a low volume of freight. The circumstances that allowed a clipper to make a round-trip to San Francisco and China in eleven months and cover her building cost and a profit were exceptional and lasted less than a decade.

Buttersworth also lived through and recorded the changes wrought by steam. Ironically, the perfection of the sailing ship coincided with the development of the technology that made it obsolete. Steam was first successfully applied shortly after 1800 in river and coastal waters, where American innovators such as J. C. Stevens spearheaded the development of the walking beam engine. A Supreme Court decision of 1824 eliminated all barriers to steam navigation on the rivers. By the time Buttersworth reached America, the passenger steamboat had replaced sail on the Hudson and inland waters and was competing in the coastal trade along the Atlantic coast, both north and south. Although passenger traffic was the first to shift, the freight business gradually followed.[33] Steamboats became faster and their performance more predictable.[34] From 1838 on, steam was introduced into naval and transatlantic ships. The sloop-of-war *Princeton* became the first screw-propelled warship, and the Collins line introduced the straight-stem steamship. Because the prevailing westerlies made steam more efficient for the westward Atlantic run, the packets were rapidly displaced after 1848, although the Black Ball line survived until 1878. The side-lever beam engine was developed in England, and eventually the compound engine and the triple expansion engine appeared. By 1870 wooden hulls had been replaced by iron and then steel, and the side wheel had been replaced by the screw propeller.

It took a century to perfect the technology of steam propulsion in oceangoing ships; large wooden hulls filled with heavy machinery were insufficiently rigid, and engines were so unreliable that sails still had to be carried. The early merchant steamers were slow, tied to their fuel supply, and unable to carry bulk cargoes. The first passenger steamers were dangerous, inconvenient, smelly, dirty, noisy, and

THE "EDWARD O'BRIEN" ENTERING PORT
24½ × 34"
Courtesy Kings Highway Trust, in care of Ropes and Gray (Boston)

Built at Thomaston, Maine, in 1863, the *Edward O'Brien* (1,803 tons) was named after a famous shipbuilder of Thomaston who died at the age of eighty-eight in 1882. The ship is depicted under reduced sail entering a South American port that may be Callao in Peru, since the boat rowing toward the ship and a building on shore, probably the customhouse, both fly the Peruvian flag. The composition is unusual in that it is an aerial view with deep perspective. Horizontal bands of light and shadow across the surface of the water open space, unite the numerous vessels, and draw the eye to the anchorage hidden behind a spit of land in the middle distance, as the view recedes into depth. The ships in the road and the houses ashore are deftly described in fine detail. The light in the sky above a bank of low-lying cloud is hard and clear and focuses the ship. Although filled with activity, the picture's overall mood is calm.

subject to extreme vibration; screw-driven ships had greater variation in draft than side-wheelers, but they required an iron hull to function efficiently, and their propellers could not be repaired at sea.[35] The first American transatlantic steam passenger ships, the *Washington* and the *Hermann*, painted by Buttersworth (plate 10), well illustrate the initial technical obstacles. Built for the Bremen run in 1847, their narrow wooden packet hulls were inherently unstable, their paddle wheels too large, and their boilers underpowered; both had to be substantially redesigned.

The change from sail to steam in America was gradual. As late as 1866 the tonnage of sail of the American merchant fleet was still six times that of steam, and sail remained competitive in the long-distance oceanic carriage of wheat, coal, sugar, and kerosene until the end of the century. The well-finished, square-rigged down-easters of 1,500 to 2,300 tons, which were developed after 1870, had huge carrying capacities, small crews, and, after 1892, steel hulls. Not until well after Buttersworth's death was sail driven from the coastal trades. The flexibility of the fore and aft rig was exploited in the schooner, which acquired up to five masts. These versatile craft even adopted steam power for hoisting cargo and sails to reduce their operating costs.

Until the Civil War, the shipyards of New York flourished, thanks to greater specialization and access to such superior materials as live oak and cedar from the South and machine-made cotton. American-built sailing ships were cheap and durable, and the local steamboats benefited from advances in technical knowledge. When Buttersworth arrived in New York, there was a solid line of yards along the East River from Grand to Twelfth streets with a few at Corlears Hook and a dry-dock section between Houston and Twelfth streets, as well as numerous lofts making rigging, sails, blocks, masts, and spars.[36] Tonnage built rose from 36,649 in 1847 to 65,521 in 1850 and 81,149 in 1854; 90 percent of the ocean packets were built in yards like those of Jacob A. Westervelt and Isaac and William Henry Webb between Fifth and Seventh streets.[37] The Novelty Works of Stillman & Allen at the corner of Dry Dock and Twelfth streets made marine engines. In 1847 New York had some 10,000 workers employed in the industry, including 2,400 carpenters, joiners, caulkers, and sawyers. In the celebrated year 1851, the clipper *Flying Cloud* (plate 17), the steamship *Pacific*, and the yacht *America* (plate 29) were all launched.

After the Civil War, the New York yards lost their edge, and the center of the industry moved to Maine, where labor and material costs were cheaper. New England had always been a major rival, and 77 percent of the square-riggers were built in Massachusetts and Maine, as were most of the coastal packets, sloops, and schooners.[38] Although Donald McKay was apprenticed to Isaac Webb in New York, he built his famous ships in Boston, where he introduced steam-powered machinery and assembly-line techniques.[39] It was New England yards, such as Bath in Maine, that, in the 1870s and 1880s, built the down-easters, and the Delaware yards that built iron ships.

During this same period, American maritime strength declined. Although the coastal trade remained in American hands behind a protective barrier first raised in 1817, the merchant marine fell by one-third while the population tripled.[40] After peaking in 1853, American tonnage declined, until by 1866 only 25 percent of foreign trade was carried in American bottoms; after 1857, British ships regained the tea trade.[41] The technical lead passed to Europe as America concentrated on railroad development and opening the interior. Whaling declined after 1876, when petroleum became a substitute for whale oil; the Suez Canal, when it was opened in 1869, was uneconomic for sailing vessels. Congress fell under the control of industrialists who were unwilling to help the merchant marine, and without federal help American shipowners could not compete in a ruthless market against subsidized British, German, and Dutch companies.[42]

This was most evident in the Atlantic. In 1840 the British Cunard line's *Britannia* initiated service to Boston, which was later extended to New York. In the same year, the Ocean Steam Navigation Company was incorporated with a mail contract subsidy and German loans to operate a comparable service to Bremen. In 1849 E. K. Collins obtained another mail subsidy to build and operate four steam liners, the *Arctic, Pacific, Baltic,* and *Atlantic,* between New York and Liverpool. The ships of the Collins line proved faster than those of Cunard, but they were more costly to build and were more frequently out of service. Their high maintenance costs and the poor quality of American coal made it impossible to run them at a profit. After the *Arctic* collided with another vessel in fog and sank with heavy loss of life, Congress refused to renew the mail subsidy in 1858 and the line was forced into bankruptcy. The railroad tycoon Vanderbilt employed two steamers on the Le Havre and Bremen routes at discounted fares in 1857, but he never instituted a regular service and was primarily interested in attracting the immigrant trade from the packets.[43]

Even though the structure and distribution of the shipping industry changed, the port of New York continued to grow. The Manhattan piers, originally constructed by the city on open pilings and leased at cheap rates, were upgraded, and the entrances to channels were marked more effectively with buoys, lighthouses, and lightships. As early as 1840 the East River had sixty-three wharves and the Hudson River fifty-three. Gradually the East River was developed far north of South Street, and though it took a long period to accomplish, the passage through Hell Gate to the Long Island Sound was eventually widened by blasting the reefs. More solid piers were built for oceanliners on both sides of the Hudson, which had greater depth close to shore than the East River, and the offices of shipping lines moved westward. In 1847 Cunard built wharves at Jersey City, and from the 1860s on Hoboken became the terminus of the German lines.[44] Much of the freight business was diverted to Brooklyn, where large warehouses were constructed.

Paradoxically, as American shipping declined and steam edged out sail, interest in recreational sailing boomed. Buttersworth was very much aware of this, and from the 1870s on he focused his attention on yachting. Sailing and racing yachts had always been a passion for those who loved the sea. Waterfront sloops raced for bets, and yacht clubs sprang up to organize competitive sailing on inland and coastal waters. New York had the Brooklyn and the Larchmont yacht clubs, though the most famous and acknowledged leader was the New York Yacht Club.[45] Racing, an integral part of maritime life, was reinforced by economic competition, gambling, patriotism, and by a love of sport. River steamboats raced each other along the inland waterways until a series of disasters ended this practice; steamers competed for the fastest transatlantic crossing time. The great race of 1866 from Sandy Hook to Cowes had a prize of $90,000, each of the three participants having put in $30,000. Captain Samuels was said to have bet most of the $7,500 he was paid to command *Henrietta*.

Yachting, like horse racing, attracted entrepreneurs and sportsmen, such as John C. Stevens, founder of the New York Yacht Club, and rich, strong-willed men such as James Gordon Bennett, founder of the New York *Herald*. Only extreme ego could provoke men to drive yachts under full sail in the appalling weather conditions of an Atlantic winter, as in 1866, when tragedy did result: *Fleetwing* was pooped and lost six men overboard, one helmsman still grasping spokes torn from the wheel.[46] Racing yachts were costly to build and maintain and were increasingly sailed by professional crews. Living and cruising at sea in luxury became fashionable even for those with no interest in seamanship. During the Gilded Age, many newly rich Americans adopted a flamboyant and aggressive life-style. Yachting became part of that life-style.[47]

Racing yachts were largely built by trial and error and developed from the pilot schooners of sixty to eighty tons.[48] The most famous was the schooner *America* (plate 29), designed by George Steers and built by a syndicate led by Stevens, but the string of thoroughbreds included *Magic, Gracie, Dauntless,* and *Volunteer* (plates 25, 26, 31, and 33). American centerboard two-masted yachts had a wide beam for stability and a shallow draft to negotiate local waters. By contrast, English yachts had a narrow hull and a deep keel. The American design proved successful, though in one extreme example, the *Mohawk* capsized in a squall. In 1884 *Puritan* (plate 36), built for a Boston syndicate by Edward Burgess, finally adopted a cutter rig, though the hull remained wide and shallow. At a less elevated level were the catboats and sloop-rigged sandbaggers of eighteen to twenty-eight feet, which developed from the fast, half-decked sloops used by New York watermen (plate 40). They carried

as much as 1,800 square feet of sail, and until the rules of racing were amended to prohibit the moving of ballast, their sandbags were shifted with each tack.

Competition was fed by rivalry that was both regional—as between New York and Boston—and international.[49] It was patriotic fervor that first sent *America* to challenge the Royal Yacht Squadron and then turned the 100-Guinea Cup into the America's Cup.[50] Although the first challenge by England did not come until 1870, the excitement generated by *America*'s victory in 1851 extended far beyond the New York Yacht Club and turned the cup into a national trophy. Subsequent races became events of international importance, and more formal rules were devised to ensure fair competition among different craft. Buttersworth lived long enough to record eight challenges as well as numerous trials, and the cup may be said to have presented him with his greatest challenge as a marine artist (plates 29 and 31).

THE BUSINESS OF ART

The growth of the American economy in mid-century was accompanied by a need for reassurance about the nation's destiny.[51] The years between 1845 and 1860 are often regarded as the high point of American art, a period when hunger for culture and consciousness of the value of art developed among the middle class as well as the elite.[52] Between 1839 and 1851, 57 percent of the population of New York visited the Art Union.[53] An influential minority, inspired by nationalistic sentiments and the belief that Americans were a chosen people, advocated and sought to advance an independent American art and culture.[54] A restless quest for self-identification expressed itself in a fondness for the didactic and the grandiose in art, typified by the epic paintings of Thomas Cole, Frederick Edwin Church, and Albert Bierstadt.

By the 1850s New York had become the center of the art market, followed by Philadelphia and Boston. In the 1860s and early 1870s, the roster of tenants at the Tenth Street Studio Building could serve as a biographical index of leading artists. Although divided by rivalry and disputes, several organizations were founded on the heels of the National Academy of Design to defend the interests and status of artists, to show their work, and to promote connoisseurship.[55] The Art Union created a market among the middle class and urged artists to improve their technique, to break with Europe, and to paint native subjects. It purchased and then distributed some 2,400 paintings by lottery until this

method of sale was declared illegal by the Supreme Court in 1852 after protests from the National Academy.[56]

After the Civil War, however, the subject matter and style of art were reshaped by new fashions and tastes. As America became a world industrial power and as foreign travel became easier, those patrons desiring to be cosmopolitan turned away from native artists and chose to buy European culture.[57] By 1876 American culture was no longer unified. During the Gilded Age, the world of high art was dominated by the fancies, ambitions, and competitive consumption of a wealthy elite. The middle class sought immediate gratification and wanted simple, domestic pictures that fitted the prevailing style of interior decoration.

Private clubs like the Salmagundi, the Urban League, and the Century were founded to promote artists and develop a market among middle-class patrons. Seth Morton Vose opened a gallery in Boston in 1850 and Michael Knoedler opened one in New York by 1857. There were probably fewer than six art dealers in New York before 1860, but their number began to grow in the 1870s. They usually supplied artists with materials and frames and exhibited and sold their works on consignment. Art supply stores, which flourished on Lower Broadway, also acted as marketing outlets; confidence tricksters held mock auctions on Broadway and the Bowery that swindled the naive. Occasionally a famous painting, such as Church's *Niagara,* was put on public exhibition for a fee.

Painting was not an established vocation, and artists had to depend on their own resources. There were a few teaching jobs for artists in New York but no public subsidies.[58] Many painters could survive only by engraving and illustration. Newspapers, magazines, and books used copper or wood engravings and lithographs for illustration, and this provided employment for many, often anonymous, artists. A professional artist had to be a businessman and salesman and price his works efficiently.[59] He could not rely on chance sales at public exhibitions, which occurred infrequently, and had to advertise his name and speciality and display his wares at his studio or in a framing shop. Studio addresses were listed in the journal *The Crayon,* and artists staged receptions and visitors' days at the Dodsworth Building on Fifth Avenue.[60] Robert Salmon sold pictures painted "on speculation" through local auctions. Even when the economy was buoyant, the market for paintings was tough, difficult to gauge, and highly competitive. Some business was lost to photographers, who worked to order; although

photography was still technically limited, stereoscopic views of exteriors became immensely popular starting in the 1850s.[61] In the 1870s volume imports of paintings from Europe presented a serious threat, and overproduction by American artists increased supply well beyond effective demand.[62] Prices fell, and pictures often had to be sold at auctions for as little as ten to twenty dollars. A national market for paintings developed very slowly.

Marine artists were even more handicapped because they were effectively excluded from the sophisticated world of fine art and the new professional institutions. They were ranked with the sign painters, engravers, and decorators of figureheads. Antonio Jacobsen began painting safes for the Marvin Safe Company, and others, such as John Connell, doubled as painters of decorations on ships, if not the ships themselves. Robert Salmon did sketches for trade cards, signboards, sternboards, and theater backdrops.[63] Martin Johnson Heade may have worked as a carriage painter, and Francis Silva was apprenticed to a sign painter and worked as a carriage painter.[64] Thomas Birch, Asher B. Durand, and Winslow Homer all worked as engravers. FitzHugh Lane began as an apprentice in the famous lithographic shop of Pendeleton and turned out trade cards and book illustrations.[65] John Frederick Kensett engraved banknotes, and W. T. Richards designed light fixtures.[66] James Hamilton did book illustrations, and Frederick Schiller Cozzens worked for the New York *Herald* and illustrated books on yachting.[67] Archibald Cary Smith was a yacht designer and builder.[68] Worthington Whittredge acknowledged "a gulf of many thousand miles between a house painter and a painter of pictures," but he began by painting houses and gravitated to boot and shoe signs, silk hats, fire wagons, and temperance banners.[69]

The depiction of ships on maps, seals, murals, and monuments as well as on canvas and panel is a practice of great antiquity. The tradition of commemorating survival at sea with an ex-voto lasted in the Mediterranean until modern times.[70] But the rapid growth of the maritime economy in the nineteenth century created a new market for portraits of merchant rather than naval ships. Builders, owners, and masters of ships, merchants, and yachtsmen wished to capture the pride of ownership and command and honor craftsmanship and design. Even those with little connection to the sea were driven by patriotism and nostalgia to acquire portraits of famous ships, often when they were a distant memory. Shipping firms placed orders for paintings as new ves-

sels were added to a fleet and used them as advertisements in travel agencies and hotels. Banks, such as Seamen's Bank of New York, and insurance companies acquired marine scenes to decorate their offices. Although foreign lines in New York employed American artists—often artists such as Fred Pansing or Jacobsen, who were of European origin—competition for commissions was international. Many American ships were painted while in foreign ports by local artists, like the Roux family in Marseille, Edouard Adam in Le Havre, or Petrus Weyts in Antwerp.[71] London, Liverpool, Copenhagen, Hamburg, and all the major Mediterranean and Chinese ports had their resident "pierhead artists."

Almost five hundred painters and engravers of marine subjects are recorded in nineteenth-century America.[72] Of these, only about forty can be regarded as artists of real distinction, and the total number includes many minor decorative illustrators rescued from obscurity because they recorded an important ship or event. But others were highly competent or even inspired on occasion, and many flourished at the regional level.[73] Many attractive paintings signed by unknown artists have also come to light as well as hundreds of anonymous portraits. The quantity of marine paintings did not exceed that of other subjects, but it is likely that some five hundred were produced each year, which would amount to about fifty thousand over the whole century. Jacobsen may have been exceptional in that he took commissions from captains who had to sail with the tide. But he painted somewhere between two to five thousand paintings and turned out a couple every three days.[74]

In New York marine artists were to be found in Brooklyn and Staten Island, though they were mostly concentrated in a specific area on both sides of the Hoboken ferry.[75] Some specialized in a particular niche: J. F. Hugo was fond of dry-dock scenes, and the Bards painted only steamboats. Every major artist had his imitators; Joseph B. Smith, for example, followed the Bards. But the range of subject matter, particularly of the more serious artists, was diverse. FitzHugh Lane, William Bradford, and Robert Salmon accepted commissions for ship portraits but were also interested in rural landscape and urban topography; Thomas Birch combined portraits, like the *America of Salem,* with port scenes and seascapes; even the landscape artist Albert Bierstadt was prepared to record ships.[76]

Although very few of Buttersworth's known paintings were pierhead portraits, he undertook many commissions, which he probably acquired by referral. In the 1850s

and 1860s West Hoboken was some distance from the active port, although Jacobsen moved there in 1880 and the New York Yacht Club was initially located in Hoboken. Buttersworth covered the regattas, and his small panel pictures, which hung in the staterooms of yachts, were almost certainly produced to order (plate 38). In some cases his patrons can be identified. The builder Tilton bought a pair of portraits, and Vernon H. Brown commissioned the *Industry,* the *Alice Ball,* and the *James Cheston.* Nichols L. McKay owned a portrait of the *Great Republic.*[77] The master of the *United States* commissioned a pair of paintings of his ship floating off a sandbar (plates 21 and 22). The prize offered by the Brooklyn Yacht Club on September 29, 1870, was two portraits of the winning yacht, *Alice,* one by Buttersworth and one by A. Cary Smith.[78] Buttersworth's painting of *Puritan* and *Genesta* in 1885 was in the collection of Catherine Spencer, whose family owned *Puritan* (plate 36).[79]

Buttersworth also benefited from the new consumer demand for lithographs and chromolithographs, exploited most successfully by lithographers Currier & Ives. The substitution of steel for copper plates and the mechanization of production after 1860 provided a cheaper alternative to hand-colored prints, and there were one hundred firms competing in New York alone by 1879.[80] Indeed, Buttersworth first obtained recognition and reached the middle-class market by working for Nathaniel Currier. He was clearly involved with many more Currier prints than bear his name.[81] Unsigned examples include the *Comet in a Hurricane*, the *Contest and America*, and several yachting scenes. In the 1870s and 1880s, some of his paintings were also brought out as undistinguished chromolithographs by Verell & Peckett and Bencke and Scott.

Buttersworth's speculative pictures were probably marketed through framers and his studio.[82] Although Buttersworth sold nine canvases to the Art Union shortly after his arrival in New York, he was neither a member nor did he exhibit at the National Academy of Design or the Brooklyn Academy; nor was he represented at the International Maritime Exhibition in Boston in 1889–1890.[83] Like Cozzens, he could probably not afford to accumulate pictures for an exhibition and had to sell continuously to provide for his family.[84] Although he painted famous engagements, like that between the *Kearsage* and the *Alabama*, he probably had a hard time during the Civil War, which was primarily a land war and provided few opportunities for marine artists.

Established artists could set their own prices.

Durand, Kensett, Hicks, and Huntington commanded $300 to $1,000 a picture, and William Hart and Shattuck averaged $60 for a small and $300 for a large picture, Tait $150 to $500, and Cropsey $40 to $200; but a standard landscape or figure, 14 by 20 inches, fetched between $40 and $60.[85] Heade's prices ranged from $35 to $67.50; in 1861–1862 he asked $20 to $35 for a small painting and $150 for a large one. In an active year his total sales were $992 with net receipts of $400, though in 1860 he made only $200.[86] The price of ship paintings, although always related to size, remained low. Bradford was selling for $25 in the 1850s, though he later received $10,000 for one painting.[87] Jacobsen sometimes charged $100 to $150, but also would sell for $25 and sometimes for $5.[88] When he came to America, Salmon sold the paintings he had brought with him for $10 to $15 apiece, and only slowly did his proceeds from private sales rise from $150 to $400 and ultimately $750.[89] At the International Maritime Exhibition of 1889–1890 the asking price for a W. B. Stubbs yacht portrait was only $25 and for his portrait of the *Tecumseh* only $35.[90] In 1888 Homer sold his famous *Eight Bells* for $400.[91]

The only contemporary prices recorded for Buttersworth's works relate to his early years and range from $20 to $50. At the Art Union in 1850 and 1852 he received $45 for a Thames shipping scene, 18 by 24 inches; $31 for a sloop-of-war, 12 by 16 inches; $22 for the steamship *Atlantic,* 12 by 16 inches; and $25 for a distant view of the Battery, 12 by 16 inches.[92] The purchasers were mainly from New York State, though one came from Ohio. As Buttersworth's reputation grew, and allowing for inflation after 1860, his prices may have improved. But he also had to cover the cost of canvas, paint, framing, packing, and shipping.[93] Heade paid between $1.50 and $35 for his frames from Vose, his brushes cost ten cents apiece, and his canvases twenty cents per square foot.[94] In order to keep a family of four in New Jersey in the 1850s, Buttersworth needed to earn at least $10.37 a week or $600 per annum according to a cost-of-living index in the New York *Daily Tribune.*[95] A ship's carpenter in 1840 was paid $2 per day, and in 1849 a laborer earned $4.25 per week; board was $3 per week, and a four-room house rented for $5.50.[96] In 1840, a longshoreman was said to earn $9 per week, a ship's painter (not a portraitist) and carver $10.50, and a copper-plate engraver $12.15.[97]

How did Buttersworth support his family and accumulate a modest estate? His wife may have worked: The wife of painter Antonio Jacobsen, for example, ran a hair-dressing business. But Buttersworth does not seem to have had any employment apart from painting. Since he could not command high prices for his pictures, at least not in the 1850s, he must have compensated by greater production, and this may explain his sometimes hurried and sketchy compositions. He must have had to sell at least 25 pictures each year to support his family. This implies that Buttersworth sold at least 1,200 pictures while he was in America, and his total output, including his English period, must have been at least 1,500 and was probably over 2,000. Approximately 880 paintings are known to exist.[98] But many others clearly have disappeared or are hidden or unnoticed in private hands. Relatively few paintings from his English period and few of those exhibited at the Art Union have so far been traced. Portrait painters usually had an output of 30 to 50 per year. Salmon took a day and a half to fourteen days to finish a picture and painted an average of 20 each year. He is known from his own inventory to have produced 1,000 paintings, but only 270 have been accounted for, and the same proportion of Heade's pictures has probably survived.[99]

Within the limitations imposed by his marine focus, Buttersworth chose a broad range of subject matter.

Although he initially gained fame with his clippers, he painted every kind of sailing ship—packets, brigs, schooners, and pilot boats. It would also be a mistake to stereotype him in later life as a painter of yachts. Although nearly half of his known pictures are of yachts, catboats, and sandbaggers, and his interest in yachting predates his migration to America, more scenes of yachting trials and races have survived because they were popular and most of them were executed later in his life, when he was in America. Since it is likely that half of his pictures have disappeared, there is no certainty about the actual distribution or relative proportions of different subjects.

His naval paintings may be underrepresented since most of them were painted during his English period. He certainly recorded many English, American, and French ships of the line, frigates, and sloops (see page 8 and plate 3), including the *Victory*, the *Britannia*, the *Collingwood*, the *Thebes*, the *Rodney*, the *Trafalgar*, the *Niagara*, and the *Chickamauga*.[100] He also painted many more steamers than is often appreciated. These range from such coastal and river craft as the *Escort* and the *Armina* (plates 12 and 13) to the *Western Metropolis* (plate 11) and a screw bark, such as the *Jeannette*.[101] His steam-powered tugboats, riverboats, and yachts are usually diminutive and introduced as secondary vessels for contrast and decorative effect (plate 35). But he painted several American and British transatlantic steamers, including the *Atlantic* of the Collins line.[102]

The small number of his surviving landscapes and portscapes may also be deceptive. They included such varied subjects as views of Chimney Rock, Grants Causeway, a moonlit fishing trip, several studies of Lake George—including the Fort William Henry Hotel favored by the Hudson River school—Lake Erie, the Hudson River, pastoral scenes with cattle, and a view of San Francisco Bay.[103] Several of his landscapes, like Salmon's, were of British scenes, including Leith Harbor, the Goodwin Sands, and Liverpool, and he continued to paint English subjects after he came to America. At the Art Union, he exhibited views of the Thames along with American harbor scenes and ships of both nations.

It is also possible that, as in Jacobsen's family, Buttersworth was helped by a son, James, who lived nearby and appears to have worked as an engraver in a watchcase factory. His son may have only finished pictures, but he may also have painted some from scratch. Approximately one-fifth of Buttersworth's known paintings are unsigned, and those that are anonymous are sometimes one of a pair or duplicates.[104] Some examples, particularly the landscapes, have the mannerisms, but not the quality, of Buttersworth's usual work, and several mediocre paintings could reasonably be attributed to his son.[105] There are variations in signature over time, but there is no obvious correlation between form of signature and quality, and no one signature can be positively identified as Butterworth's son.[106]

Buttersworth had to respond to a competitive market, which determined what he painted. American artists were often unfairly accused of sacrificing artistic to commercial principles, but art was a commodity and there were more marine artists than the market required. Buttersworth had to take the commissions he was offered, please his patrons, copy his own work, and cater to popular taste in prints. His work reflects both the changes that occurred in the shipping industry and what others thought was important or wished to commemorate or remember. When he chose his own subjects, Buttersworth did not consult his inner muse but selected what would sell. He made a niche for himself as a yachting artist when peace at sea and the growth of photography reduced demand for merchant and naval ship portraits. "Most of our artists," reflected a contemporary, "paint to live, hoping perhaps the time may come when they may live to paint."[107] Buttersworth's priority was economic survival, a fact that limited his range of options.

TECHNIQUE

The essential elements of Buttersworth's approach to painting can be ascertained from a study of his methods—his borrowings from other artists, his choice of medium and scale, his sequence of execution, draftsmanship, brushwork, palette, and visual memory.[108] Since no written evidence survives of what he learned from other artists, their influence has to be deduced solely from his actual paintings. Caution has to be exercised in generalizing about his technique, which varies between different pictures as well as periods; some are executed *alla prima,* and others are glazed and highly finished. But it is possible to describe how Buttersworth expressed himself in paint and to explain his distinctive manner.

A marine artist faces three particular obstacles. First, since the sky features prominently in any seascape, the marine artist, like the rural landscape artist, has to capture the shape and structure of clouds, the transitory effects of weather, and the weight and movement of invisible air. Second, the portraitist needs an intimate knowledge of ship design—the shape of hulls, rigging, and fittings. Ships were complex pieces of machinery with as much as three miles of rope, blocks, lines, and canvas. To represent them three-dimensionally required precise draftsmanship and a firm grasp of perspective. They had to settle deep enough in the water to support their weight and, when moving, generate the right wave motion and wake. The set of the sails and the angle of heel had to be consistent with the strength and direction of the wind.[109]

Third and most important, the seascapist must master the demanding task of painting seawater, which is both solid and fluid, translucent and reflective of light. The sea is always in motion and varies in texture and consistency according to depth, wind and weather conditions, time of year, and the light in which it is viewed. The surface characteristics of water and the action of waves vary with currents and the wind, their distance from the shore, whether they are confined to narrow inlets or breaking on rocks or open sand. Rolling waves progress in a repetitive and orderly manner and tend to be evenly spaced until the plane becomes steeper with reduced depth. The arch of a breaking wave is momentarily powerful and massive, but the sharp-edged crest eventually dissolves in turmoil, the weight of water creating bouncing masses of foam and a wild scattering of spray. The color of the sea also changes as frequently as its form. It usually appears to be gray green when nearby and gray blue in the distance where it reflects the sky. Given these variations, the appearance of the water in the Solent, for example, differs markedly from that of New York Harbor.

By the nineteenth century the specific requirements of marine painting had established tenacious conventions, stock motifs, and standard visual tricks that were universally followed. The basic compositional format had originally been adapted from landscape painting by the Dutch. Vessels were arranged in a pyramidal structure or along a low horizon to create a sense of perspective. The foreground was usually dark, because water appears smoother in the distance and less light is reflected by moving water. A device originally introduced when pictures were conceived as windows, the foreground established a viewpoint for the spectator and a stage for the action. It was commonly defined by a barrel, a rowboat or dory with dripping oars, fishermen tending their nets, wheeling gulls, buoys, or drifting wreckage. Horizontal bands of alternating sunlight and shadow across the surface of the water marked off space, as the view receded into depth and drew the eye to sunlit sails and hulls in the middle distance; zigzag shadows united scattered vessels.[110]

In a portrait, the ship was usually portrayed broadside, slightly off center and parallel to the picture plane, with other vessels to lend balance, interest, and animation to the design, and—until it fell out of favor in the nineteenth century—an alternative view from the stern. Ships were shown traveling in a horizontal path following the natural movement of the eye; head-on or three-quarter views were more rare. The port side was preferred and a leeward view, because in a windward view the contours of the sails and the rigging were less visible. Usually the ship was on a level plane with translucent water thrown up by the bow, though the angle of heel was also adjusted to show the sails more effectively. There was a standard composition for storm and fair-weather pictures, in which the position of the ship and the waves varied little.

James Buttersworth must have been taught initially by either his father or grandfather, and he was clearly exposed to and influenced by their work. Since the work of the two Thomases has not as yet been clearly differentiated, determining their relative impact on James is difficult. But he is more likely to have imitated Thomas Senior, who

appears to have been the more accomplished artist. Thomas Senior painted in a formalistic style and preferred a gray tonality with dark overcast skies and muddy dark green seas shading off to creamy white.[111] Buttersworth adopted Thomas's palette of blue and green grays, light tan, and purple, though his color range was broader and less monotone and his palette much warmer; he also relied more on glazing to obtain a better finish. He imitated Thomas's smooth modeling of ships and his efforts to re-create the play of light on waves, his manipulation of light and shadow to suggest movement through the water, and his dramatic cloud formations (plate 14). The influence of Thomas is most evident when several vessels are placed in open seas engaged in related actions (plate 1). Buttersworth painted the same ships and subjects, including various versions of a stern chase in which a smuggler or privateer in flight is fired on by a pursuing ship.[112] Unlike Thomas, however, James Buttersworth rarely painted in watercolor, and he eventually developed beyond lumpy and regularized seas.

Thomas, of course, was himself influenced by eighteenth-century English marine artists, including Dominic Serres and Charles Brooking, who in turn had borrowed from the Dutch engravers and painters, particularly the two

Van der Veldes.[113] Any artist trained during the 1830s was exposed to both the selective naturalism and realism of the Dutch as well as to French and Italian romanticism and Turner's impressionism. Salmon, for example, was influenced by Samuel Scott and Canaletto, by Ibbetson and the Scottish landscapists, as well as by Turner.[114] Dutch influence is noticeable in some of Buttersworth's paintings, probably acquired from prints or filtered through English models (see page 13). Buttersworth had a similar sense of the continuity of space and the interaction of light and water; he also employed delicately modulated gray washes for atmospheric effects and favored lively seas and banks of clouds with patches of clear sky.[115] Even so, he never emulated the intense hues or the sobriety and grandeur of classic Dutch painting, and he was not trained in Dutch technique as Bradford and A. Cary Smith were. Nor was Buttersworth captivated by Italian light, by the decorative elegance of Vernet, the crystalline forms of the Pre-Raphaelites, or the restless spontaneity of the European romantic tradition.[116] As his treatment of weather illustrates, he was firmly rooted in the English marine tradition, which emphasized a literal approach to subject matter.[117]

When Buttersworth arrived in New York, the dominant school of American landscape painting was romantic realism, which drew on earlier European traditions. The realistic pastoral was borrowed from seventeenth-century Holland with strong atmospheric effects gleaned from English landscape. The exhibition of the Pre-Raphaelites in 1857, with their emphasis on bright local color at the expense of tonal modulation to avoid artificiality, reinforced the views of the early Hudson River school artists.[118] But American artists were positing a different attitude to the objective world and were particularly committed to the exploration of light and atmosphere without any disintegration of terrestrial form. In the 1850s Kensett and Gifford, the second generation of the Hudson River school, discarded Cole's broad painterly style and formal large-scale compositions and introduced crisp, light color with unifying tones.[119] The luminists went further and rejected the diagonal pull of classical composition and favored horizontal paintings of water or recumbent terrain that emphasized the plane of the picture surface.[120] They used minute tonal modulations to negate the idea of paint and mimic the radiance of cool, crystalline, gleaming hard light. Their focus on the play and power of light, rather than on the subject per se, developed from and in many respects represents the last phase of the

Hudson River school; Cropsey and Church can be regarded as atmospheric luminists.[121]

Kensett returned from Europe in 1847, and Heade was in New York in 1859 and 1867. Although it is unlikely that Buttersworth had any personal contact with these painters, he must have seen the work both of the romantic realists and the luminists at the Art Union in 1850. Their influence must not be exaggerated. Buttersworth was never a romantic in the sense of unrestrained emoting or being drawn to sensational and tragic incidents. His work was not didactic or spiritual or grandiose. But he had a muted romantic sensibility and a Wordsworthian awareness of the intimate relationship between the artist and nature, which is evident in his handling of light on water. The theatricality of the breaks of light in his clouds and the stylized melodrama of his storms recall the work of Thomas Cole. He often employed chiaroscuro and stark contrasts of light in the water for visual impact, as in the *Eagle* (plate 18); he sometimes lit his main subject and left the other vessels in shadow.[122] Like the Hudson River school artists, Buttersworth observed nature objectively and depicted his seascapes with a polished and meticulous realism.[123] He favored light, imperceptible brushstrokes, precise detail, and a smooth finish. He honored the impersonal status, integrity, and unbroken identity of the object, and he emphasized surface likeness and durability.

Buttersworth did not reject anecdotal detail or raise the conceptual above the pictorial, as did the luminists, who regarded light as a revelatory eternal essence in opposition to matter. He never dissolved objective form in light but clarified it sharply. On the other hand, he did reject topographical elaboration and downplay the human presence. He modulated his transitions from light to dark, and some of his skies, though never menacing, have a surreal quality (plates 14 and 26). His black storm scenes have similarities with Heade's famous *Coming Storm* of 1859, as does his occasional downplay of foreground and his central axis of sunlight. His sunsets have parallels with Gifford and Kensett, and his brightly colored skies over dark seas recall Bricher and Francis Silva.[124] Like Elisha Taylor Baker, he combined luminist techniques with the ship's portrait.[125]

Although there is no hard evidence that Buttersworth had contact with any marine artists in America, it was a small world, and he must have encountered them in the normal course of business, at regattas and exhibitions and on the waterfront, and seen examples of their work. Buttersworth was a neighbor of Jacobsen, who also lived initially on Eighth Avenue in Manhattan before moving in 1880 to 705 Palisades Avenue in West Hoboken, where he was acquainted with Buttersworth, according to Jacobsen's son.[126] The illustrator, lithographer, and painter Andrew Melrose, who emigrated to New York from Scotland around 1856, also lived for a time in West Hoboken, and Hoboken had an artist colony.[127] Edward Moran was in New York between 1872 and 1878, and the Bards, Cozzens, and Fred Pansing all lived in the waterfront area on both sides of the Hudson and probably socialized with one another.[128] Buttersworth's picture of the *Narragansett* has some similarities with a Bard painting.[129] Lane was in New York in 1850 and exhibited a sunset scene at the Art Union in 1852. Marine artists probably exchanged ideas and sometimes painted the same events. Van Beest collaborated with Bradford at a New York Yacht Club regatta that was also attended by Lane.

Buttersworth had little in common with either the artists of the Hoboken school or with those, like the Bards, who followed the American limner tradition of linear and tactile identification.[130] He had little interest in topography and was not a Turneresque painter of impressionistic scenes, like James Hamilton of Philadelphia. The three American marine artists who are most likely to have influenced him

are Salmon, Lane, and Bradford (the latter two were influenced both by Salmon and by each other). Buttersworth did not freeze his action and close his space, like Salmon, but he favored tight handling, minute realization, and a hard-edged finished technique (plate 44). From Lane he may have acquired his interest in light and his inclination to push the distant horizon into space.[131] Like Bradford, Buttersworth preferred close-in views and blue and green tonalities.[132]

Buttersworth did not confine himself to the conventional broadside portrait parallel to the canvas but experimented with different angles—an approaching bow, a receding stern, and a three-quarter view. His ship portraits are usually placed in realistic settings with complementary vessels and under a variety of weather conditions (see page 4 and plates 3 and 7). Buttersworth often introduced anecdotal incidents to add interest and produced some purely narrative paintings, which usually tell a dramatic story of a rescue or fire (plates 21–24, and 42). Although he sometimes filled a canvas with a ship, he never attempted close-up views of life on or between decks or on the waterfront. His figures were small and impressionistic and painted from a distance.[133] He eschewed whaling and fishing subjects and tended to avoid naval engagements.[134] He showed no interest in heroic or panoramic compositions, studies of rocks or marshes, beach scenes, or pure studies of the sea. The shore was invariably depicted from a viewpoint at sea and rarely in winter, mist, or at night. Buttersworth did include exotic locations from Havana to Palermo and occasionally produced a detailed port scene (see page 16 and plates 44 and 45). But his landmarks were usually sketched in fairly casually in his shipping scenes, and his portscapes were not really topographical (plates 46 and 47). They served simply as a backdrop—his principal focus was always ship, sea, and sky.

Seascapes usually required a rectangular format, and Buttersworth produced very few vertical or oval pictures. Among the exceptions are his drawings of the *Aurora*, which show a proposed vertical with an oval top, and one pair of miniatures.[135] Buttersworth did, however, tend to de-emphasize the horizontal. Whereas Heade and Bricher favored a height-to-width ratio of 2:1, Buttersworth's most common ratio was 1.5:1, and some of his paintings have a ratio of 1.1:1.[136] For convenience, he often used standard commercial lengths of canvas and board. His few low rectangular panels were probably intended to hang in the staterooms of yachts (plates 38 and 39). Buttersworth painted in a great variety of

sizes and often reproduced the same picture in different dimensions, as in his *View of Nassau* (plate 46) and his storm scenes.[137] There are a few monumental examples, like the *Western Metropolis* (plate 11), but he preferred small, unpretentious, and intimate cabinet-style pictures. The complexity of the subject did not determine size; he often condensed a detailed picture into a small compass (plates 13, 40, 41, and 44). Indeed, his talent for miniaturization distinguishes him from most other American marine artists, and some of his best pictures are small in scale.

Although on occasion Buttersworth utilized metal and even a cigar-box lid, he usually painted on canvas, artist's board or millboard, and panel. Most of his canvases are not fine-grained and appear to be commercially sheared and prepared, though the tacking edges suggest that he sometimes primed them himself. Buttersworth declined to use gesso, and when he painted on board, the underlying nodules give texture to the painting. But he usually sought to obtain a smooth and uniform surface that would not absorb paint. As a primer and binder to which his paint could adhere he appears to have used animal glue diluted in water. A neutral ground was applied to set the overall tonal quality and was sometimes allowed to show through the superimposed layers of paint. He used a thin, opaque wash that was sometimes a gray-brown monochrome in warm tones, but could also be an earthy reddish brown or pink, yellow, blue, and even purple. Judging by some examples of what appears to be the original varnish, he used a standard resin.

Although a few pencil sketches and watercolors survive, the medium he favored was oil.[138] In the 1860s research into chromatic color in New York had produced chemical-based pigments that were more brilliant than natural materials; but Buttersworth, presumably for financial reasons, tended to use the cheaper commercial paints, and sometimes his paintings give the impression that he felt obliged to use every bit of paint on his palette. In order to manipulate his paint fluidly and achieve a smooth finish, he thinned his pigments markedly with oil and sometimes used varnish in his intermediary layers. He painted fat and rich, with a high ratio of medium to pigment. In many but not all of his pictures, he worked from light to dark; he laid in his cool middle tones and shadows and then superimposed a succession of transparent films of darker pigment over the lighter underpaint. By means of these glazes he was able to separate color from form and achieve a warm luminosity and dense atmospheric depth.

Buttersworth generally employed a light and subdued palette of pale greens, grays, and blues, and he favored a few dominant blended and tinted colors in reserved hues with little body and carefully controlled modulations of value. His general color scheme has great variety and a natural prettiness that catches the eye.[139] He sometimes spiked his skies with hotter pigments of red, yellow, and even purple and suffused them with an iridescent medley of bright colors. But he usually restrained his color sensations and was never as fiery as Church. Because he used viscous paint in thin layers, there was a high degree of saturation proportionate to color. Grays and yellows prevail in his skies, and blues and greens in his seas, with a balance of complementary warm and cool colors. In his more elaborate seascapes, his skies combine pale lavender with a pearl gray overall tone, and his water is a jade green (plates 30 and 46). In his painting of *Magic* (plate 25), a mass of yellowy brown clouds edged with pink and red and interspersed with patches of clear blue frames the dispersed yachts.

Buttersworth, particularly in his early paintings, used sharply polarized colors and chiaroscuro to describe form and to secure dramatic effects; his transitions between light and dark color could be abrupt.[140] Even so, adjacent areas of color are usually imperceptibly merged by careful blending, and he relied on nuances of tone rather than on flat patterns of light and dark. He shaded his colors in subtle gradations by adding white and black and by combining different hues. A gradual transition occurs in his sky and water from gray to green and blue tones. The clouds in his storm scenes have dark middle tones, and the lenticular clouds in his evening seascapes reflect the red tones of the setting sun. In his *View of Nassau* (plate 46), variations in the intensity of tones create frothy clouds whose volume is gradually reduced until the sky clears. In his study of *Flying Cloud* (plate 17), delicate gray tones tinted with white convey the interaction of light and vapor.

Thanks to careful priming, proper drying, and varnishing, most of Buttersworth's known pictures have survived in good condition. Some of those painted on artist's board have sunk—the paint medium has been absorbed by the underlayer to produce a matte surface. A greater transparency is to be expected, as the refractory index of the medium increases with age and moves closer to the underlying sensitive film of pigment. Other paintings have discolored, darkened, or cracked with time or have been weakened by injudicious cleaning. In some cases, the oil

and resin have yellowed, and the weave of the canvas is visible. Few pentimenti have surfaced, and in most cases Buttersworth's paint has adhered well and retained its strength of color.

Buttersworth's draftsmanship is tight, precise, and economical. The uniformity of line and shading in his drawings for the Dauntless Club suggests that he would have been a successful engraver.[141] Most of his Currier prints were based on his original paintings but were engraved and sometimes substantially modified by Charles Parsons and Francis F. Palmer; when his signature appears on the stone, however, he may have been directly involved in their production (plates 7, 9, 29, and 43). His brushstrokes were usually small and unobtrusive, fluid, facile, and unbroken. He manipulated impasto selectively to impart intensity to his brushwork, often raising his ships in thicker paint and even glazing over the impasto. But he preferred to apply a thin skin of liquid paint, and there was little texture in his painted surface. Occasionally, as with the edges of his clouds, he would paint wet on wet and let his colors run (plate 25). His light touch and skillful glazing eliminated all signs of the brush and created an anonymous surface. Because his brushstroke was specific, he was able to execute paintings rapidly, with simplicity and directness, and there are few signs of correction or extensive reworking.

Buttersworth understood the refractive and reflective properties of light and how it is absorbed. He did not restrict himself to a particular time of day or weather condition, though he showed little interest in night scenes. He alternated between depictions of a humid atmosphere with stormy, overcast skies and clear sunny days in which the whole canvas is suffused with a brilliant, hard light, which does not come directly from the sun but is reflected by the sky (plates 3, 11, 27, 46, and 47). At other times he did not distribute light evenly over the whole composition but concentrated it at a specific point, though it was blended progressively into deepening, cool, transparent shadows (plates 40, 41, and 45). He allowed subdued light to filter through the clouds from the corners or sides of the picture from an unspecified source or from below the horizon. Light bounces off sails and gleaming hulls and is reflected by the water. He frequently used backlighting to silhouette his vessels, often at sunset when the sun was lower and redder. This created a light top plane and a darker side plane and foreground. The *Washington* and the *Hermann*, the *Western Metropolis*, the *Armina* (plates 10, 11, and 13), the *Rescue of the Crew of a Sloop*, the *North Point* are all silhouetted against a dark sea and an illuminated horizon. But he also reversed this format and has a dark atmosphere and a light sea. His ships are sometimes silhouetted against dark clouds, and in his storm scenes Buttersworth dramatically juxtaposed areas of light and shadow (plates 15–18).

Buttersworth usually adopted the quintessential composition of the marine painter. Most of his pictures have a low horizon and vantage point, a deep foreground of dark waves, parallel bands of light and shadow, and a spacious format. There is always water in the foreground, even in his landscapes, and the viewer is often invited to identify with the spectators in the picture.[142] In his portraits, the ship is the focus of attention and occupies the most space, usually in an off-center location in the middle ground with secondary vessels traveling in different directions to balance the composition and a lighthouse, seashore, or port in the distance. Typical examples are his portraits of *Architect*, *Witchcraft*, and *Western Metropolis* (see page 4 and plates 6 and 11). Buttersworth did not always arrange his pictures in a pyramidal format or on an x-axis of two long diagonals to emphasize the center. Sometimes his composition is L-shaped, the ship providing the vertical and horizontal lines on one side of the canvas; sometimes S- or Z-shaped with a series of ships or landmarks linked from top to bottom in a zigzag pattern or with a breakwater curving into the picture plane (plates 5 and 23).[143] His yacht races often have a circular pattern with a buoy or lightship marking the center around which the competitors turn (plates 26, 32, and 34). He constantly varied the traditional devices for setting a scene. In his storm scenes, he shortened the foreground and eliminated the horizon; in his fair-weather scenes, the monotony of the horizon is relieved by foreshortening vessels (see page 1 and plates 27, 34, and 35). He also mixed together many different types of vessels for decorative interest and to introduce contrasts of form.

Buttersworth left no sketchbooks that might serve to establish the order in which he constructed a painting, but he clearly had a consistent method. When painting from life, he probably drew sketches, like those of the 1851 yachts in the *Dauntless* pictures, and then blocked out the main composition in outline on the prepared canvas with pencil, charcoal, or chalk: that is, the main shapes, the horizon line in relation to the vessels, and the fore-, middle, and background. Next he mapped out the sea and sky in a flat color, leaving an area of ground to represent shadows and reflections and give texture to the surface water. Then he built up his glazes. Since the drying time for each layer must have been considerable, he probably worked on several canvases at once using the same palette and treating the same subject from a slightly different perspective. In some paintings dirt is detectable between glazes, which suggests that he left pictures for a time and then returned to them later. The details of rigging and superstructure as well as tonal adjustments were probably added last, together with the highlighting and accents. Unlike many portraitists, Buttersworth did not just fill in the background after completing the ship—he always considered the sea and sky to be integral parts of the painting.

Buttersworth always grouped his subjects, painting the same ship many times. There are three paintings of *Dreadnought,* several of *America,* and many versions of famous yachts like *Dauntless, Magic,* and *Puritan* (plates 25, 26, 29, and 31–36)—though he never sought to emulate Jacobsen, who is alleged to have duplicated two hundred versions of the *Olympic.* Buttersworth's rowboats and secondary vessels are often simply transposed from one canvas to another. Sometimes the ship and setting are virtually identical except for changes in position and direction (plates

15–17).[144] Frequently he would paint a series of pictures with the same background and composition, slightly varying the ships or the weather or the angle of view. One such example is his set of small paintings of the British fleet in Gibraltar, in which the ships are depicted at anchor, in a storm, and from slightly different points of the compass.[145] His handling of spray and dramatic clouds also shows a certain repetition. In his racing scenes, he often placed different craft in essentially the same narrative action. In other cases, he painted exact replicas, such as his study of *Four Yachts in a Storm,* the *Gallia,* and *Puritan* and *Genesta* (plates 20, 36, and 42).

There are several possible explanations for this high degree of duplication. Buttersworth may have wanted to keep an example for himself or may have been unwilling to discard anything salable. He may also have turned out several versions of a picture that had attracted attention and that he was asked to repeat. In some cases, he improved his technique in successive versions. His storm scenes can be placed in a clear sequence as he experimented with variations of the sky and wave structure (plates 14–18). Of course, most marine artists, including Thomas Buttersworth, painted many duplicates.[146] Lane copied one picture from another, as well as sequential pictures.[147] James Buttersworth had

several different categories of complementary skies and seas, not just a stereotype.

To what extent did Buttersworth paint from life? In the heroic tradition of painting, the artists Vernet and Turner had themselves lashed to a mast during a storm for artistic inspiration, and W. T. Richards allegedly became a marine artist after a stormy crossing in 1867 in a paddle-wheeler when he witnessed the power of the sea.[148] Reynolds Beal purchased a yacht as a floating studio.[149] Buttersworth certainly had an intimate familiarity with his subject matter. He knew the construction and rigging of ships and their posture at sea. He had obviously crossed the Atlantic and had experience of the sea and meteorological changes. When painting a newly built ship or yacht that had not yet been recorded, he undoubtedly viewed and sketched the ship. He probably went to visit famous ships in the port of New York, such as the *Great Republic* before it burned, and he must have attended the regattas and have been invited on board yachts to sketch.

He was, however, not a plein-air painter. Outdoor light changes too quickly for more than a sketch, and Buttersworth was primarily a studio painter relying on memory and imagination.[150] He continued to paint English subjects after he came to New York, and certainly copied his own paintings and those of other artists. His painting of a convoy in Liverpool's Mersey River in 1866 is identical to a painting by Samuel Walters.[151] He must have consulted engravings, lithographs, and illustrations in magazines and possibly even ship models, photographs, and silhouettes. The aesthetic of photography attracted many artists (Bierstadt, Lane, Bradford, Cozzens, Eakins, and Homer all practiced photography) until a reaction against the medium set in after 1880, and artists reverted in self-defense to subjectivity.[152] It is conceivable that Buttersworth visited Saratoga Springs, the Fort William Henry Hotel, and the Bronx River, but not Portugal, Boston, Palermo, Nassau, the Savannah River, or Aberdeen. It is clear that he never saw many of the ships he painted, and some of his clippers were probably painted retrospectively. Some vessels were entirely imaginary.[153] This was a common practice. Hamilton drew on English and Dutch engravings, and Lane copied one of Hamilton's two portraits of the *America*, though his picture of the famous race of 1851 was based on a sketch by one of the crew.[154]

Buttersworth clearly acquired much of his technique from earlier and contemporary English and American marine artists, whether directly through instruction or indirect-

ly by observing and copying their works. Although it is difficult to demonstrate specific influences, and analogies must be treated with circumspection, Buttersworth responded to an artistic tradition. He also deviated from convention and developed his own skills by trial and error. His style had matured by the late 1860s, and he was unaffected by the fundamental changes in approach and multiplicity of styles that appeared after 1870. He continued to paint in a tightly detailed mode with clear pictorial definition even as painterly suggestiveness and self-expressionism emerged along with a looser palette, thicker pigment and heavier brushstrokes, rough texture, greater spontaneity, and a more subjective response. Although Buttersworth inevitably repeated himself, he covered a wide range of subjects. His early pictures do lack assurance, but he eventually became technically proficient in what was a particularly difficult field, and he was able to combine exactness with imagination.

CRITICAL APPRECIATION

How important was Buttersworth as an artist? How does his grasp of design, form, light, composition, and perspective compare with that of his peers? A formal analysis of his style must take into account changes over time as well as variations of quality within his work. It is difficult, however, to distinguish between periods because there are few dated paintings, such as the *Gallia*, to serve as benchmarks (plate 20).[155] It is difficult to date a painting according to subject matter, because ships were often painted long after they were built. It is also imprecise to date a painting according to style, as Buttersworth reverted to his early style late in his life. It should be taken into consideration that Buttersworth could not afford to paint only masterpieces. He sometimes had to cater to demand and dash off routine, perfunctory, and formulaic paintings to sustain a minimum level of sales.

Buttersworth has been credited with an early, middle, and late style, and differences certainly exist between paintings produced before and after his emigration to America.[156] Some of his earlier pictures have a more rudimentary sense of perspective, blander skies, a congested composition, fuzzy seas, monochrome or poorly blended color, and weak tonality.[157] It is true that many of his persistent mannerisms—the illumination of the hull, the highlighted foam over the bow, the angle of heel, and the hole in the clouds—occur early in his career (plate 38), but they were continually refined, and his style did not mature until the

1860s. His *Expedition to Paraguay*, for example, experiments unsuccessfully with the reflection of sails in the water, a device he later discarded. His experience in America may have encouraged him to develop seas and skies that were quite different from those of his English mentors.

The major parts of the ship in a commissioned portrait—the line of the hull, the masts, the spars, the standing and running rigging, and the sails, whether set or furled—had to be sufficiently accurate to convince the purchaser. The original patrons of marine art had been general collectors who were primarily concerned with style and mood, but the captains, owners, and builders who assumed this role were interested in accuracy rather than imagination. The traditional ship portraitist, the Bards for example, drew to scale like a marine architect, albeit in two dimensions. The pierhead artist carefully recorded every detail down to the clear lettering of the name, the figurehead, deck, gunwales, wheelhouse, pennants, and houseflags. Sometimes an artist was given a specific position, weather conditions, and points of sailing—whether tacking, close hauled, or hove to in a storm. Of course, patrons also wanted their ships romanticized and shown in their best light. The paintwork was always fresher and the ships larger than life.

To a certain extent Buttersworth complied with these conventions. He employed a fineness of detail and even conveyed the texture of the seamed sails and rigging as well as activity on board, like reefing sails during a storm. He observed each ship as a unique object with its own life-force, as though painting a horse or a man. Buttersworth's paintings certainly display acute and astute observation and a salty veracity. He had a searching eye for the effects of weather on waves and ships, the rise of wind and the force of a gale, the shifting of cloud, the changes of season and barometric pressure, and the difference between dry and humid air. But he also ignored or suppressed unwanted information and was more interested in appearance than in reality. He compromised the factual record in order to produce an attractive picture. Buttersworth took considerable artistic license in depicting the headings of ships and the direction of the wind (plate 29). His buoys, lighthouses, headlands, and landmarks, like Castle Williams and Castle Garden, were intended as identifying devices and were stereotyped pictorial motifs and not topographically precise (plates 10 and 28). Much of his detail, like the cannon salutes, was included for decorative interest rather than for documentary purposes.

All art is artifice, however skillfully this may be concealed. No pigment can convey the exact colors of nature, and no artist can, even if he wishes, copy what he sees.[158] Painting is an optical illusion, and it is the mind, not the retina, that distinguishes sea from sky. It is Buttersworth's perception of the world and not the accuracy of factual observation that animates his paintings. His realism was not literal illustration, but was achieved by contrivance. He selected scenes for his brush that were naturally ordered in the visible world but were transformed by his imagination into a fictive world. Excessive concern with detail and the labored representation of facts would have cluttered his picture and cramped his style. Buttersworth altered the proportions of his vessels, elongated their sails, and raised their bows above their sterns to achieve dramatic intensity.[159] He sought to create an impression, not to offer a photographic likeness. A photograph captures the whole image at a split second and is indiscriminate, whereas a painting can suggest even the snap of a sail and ropes, the shrieking of the wind, and the smell of salt, timber, and canvas. Buttersworth's objective was fidelity rather than precision.

He certainly had a striking eye and was an impeccable draftsman who modeled tightly and crisply. The graphic character and optical realism of ship portraits required a firm grasp of linear structure. Buttersworth delineated the complex contours of hulls and rigging with clarity and without clutter or confusion; his ship portraits have bold, hard silhouettes even in storms. His fluid, economical, and dexterous brushstrokes did give his skies an expressive delicacy. But Buttersworth emphasized particular rather than general shapes and relied on outline as much as on color, shading, highlighting, and an incisive but discreetly applied impasto. His modeling shines through the superimposed, saturated local colors. His forms stand out sharply with few blurred edges and are not subordinated to light and atmosphere. Buttersworth also focuses his subject and emphasizes its intrinsic visual interest through the meticulous selection of minute, incidental details. By direct and concentrated observation he captures the tension of the sails and rigging and the sheeting action of waves in sequence. He recognized the importance of pictorial design. The contrasting shapes of vessels, clouds, and waves are arranged in a network of decoratively balanced light and dark patterns. His billowing sails are echoed by scudding clouds and by the white crests of foam at the interstices of his waves; the *United States* is echoed by an accompanying pilot boat (plate 22).

Buttersworth was more skilled at conveying water than landmasses, which he tended to depict softly without volume or depth. His renderings of icebergs, the Rock of Gibraltar, or the island of Ischia lack tactile physicality and tangible concreteness.[160] His ships, on the other hand, appear light and buoyant in relation to the density of the sea. His waves rise and fall with a fluid actuality, and his cumulus, stratus, and nimbus clouds have an accurately vaporous and ephemeral texture (see pages 4 and 13 and plates 5, 7–9, 20, and 30). His sails hang under their own weight or are taut with wind, and he captured the fragile structure of scattered drops of spray lofted by the wind.

No rigorous or sophisticated interlocking mathematical structure or abstract pattern underlies his paintings, as with Lane and Salmon. Buttersworth did not feel obliged to adopt a formal, rigid structure, and he sometimes juxtaposed unrelated objects or partially intercepted and subdued an object from whim rather than by design. Many of his canvases are crowded, and the vessels obstruct one another or extend beyond the edge of the canvas.[161] His ships off the Eddystone lighthouse not only overhang the picture, but the eye is drawn to the lighthouse rather than to the vessels.[162] He occasionally added fussy, decorative detail without thought for its effects on the composition. But Buttersworth certainly knew how to choose, order, and manipulate elements in his compositions and how to equalize light and dark masses (see pages 1 and 4 and plates 13, 18, 20, 28, and 34). His ships off Belem Castle and his topsail schooner *Little John* are well positioned.[163] As his style developed, he attained a more gracious balance between sea and sky, and his ships were more effectively integrated into the setting. His pictures also acquired greater cohesion. The sky, through reflection, is related to the sea and different areas of color focus the action. Vessels are separated by water, but linked by physical tension, by a shared direction of wind and wave. Visual analogies are provided by highlights of the same pigment (plate 40). The oscillation of waves and movement to and from the shore introduces a rhythm and flow that bind together and unify the composition (plate 25).

Buttersworth's construction could be quite complex. He accepted the primacy of the horizontal, and his low shorelines and striated clouds accentuate the length of his ships, as in his *View of Boston*.[164] An open foreground, anchored by an object or an event, puts the viewer at the waterline; diagonal sweeps with subtle horizontal alignments define and open up space within the picture and lead the eye casually outward along a corridor of water or a line of sails toward the infinite horizon. But the severity of this dominating line is modified by juxtaposing distant ships and by the vertical relief of masts, rigging, and soaring clouds. Sometimes the spread sails and their flat reflections echo the horizon line, and sometimes they cut diagonally from corner to corner to emphasize speed (plates 27, 36, and 37). The ship is the organizing element and pyramids out into three-dimensional space. The rounded and curvilinear shapes of the hulls serve as a counterpoint to the rising points of sails (see pages 4 and 13 and plates 7–9, 26, and 31). The vessels are locked into the plane of water by diagonal reflections and short vertical accents. The crests of the waves balance the lateral lines of *The Clipper Flying Cloud off Cape Horn* (plate 17). The visual interest of the composition is further enhanced by imaginative grouping and by turning the axis of vessels, which sail diagonally on different planes rather than just parallel to the picture plane (see page 1).[165] Secondary vessels are judiciously placed asymmetrically to bisect and interrupt the horizon. In the storm pictures, there is usually no division between sea and sky, which are bound together in a gray haze; the ships are swallowed by patterns of clouds and waves that merge at the horizon (plates 15 and 42).

Although there is some distortion and lack of proportion in his early pictures, Buttersworth became a master of both linear and atmospheric perspective.[166] He created a visual sense of depth and distance through a progressive diminution in the scale of his vessels. The eye does not move toward a vanishing point in the distance, and the lines of the ships in the middle ground extend laterally beyond the canvas. But the plane of the water recedes diagonally, and objects in the fore- and middle ground serve as stepping-stones to direct the eye toward the soft line of the horizon.[167] Sometimes the foreground is abbreviated, and hulls and vessels are foreshortened to focus attention. He shows the stern of a ship pulling away from the foreground or the bow forward, as in his *New York Yacht Club Race* (see page 1) or the steamer *Egypt*. His sense of atmospheric perspective was equally subtle, and his color values become subtly darker and cooler as they recede (plate 26).[168] Buttersworth exploited the relative clarity of near and far objects and the optical effects of contrasting light and shadow on angular sails and cloud formations. The colors of his sky change at different altitudes and shift to gray blue toward the horizon.

This palpable representation of atmosphere creates a convincing illusion of pictorial space and helps the paintings' sense of narrative. Neither sea nor sky has clearly defined boundaries. Many pictures have no vertical masses on the sides to define the middle distance or frame the action. But darkened lateral edges do rise from the shaded foreground. In his storm scenes, Buttersworth achieved a domed effect through his color arrangement and tonal contrasts. The *Young America*, stern out of the water, is framed by black clouds mirrored by the sea; in the *Gallia*, the sky forms an arch echoed in the waves (plates 16 and 20). There is no vacuum of open sea space, which is instead organized, constricted, and filled by the compact mass of the ships and clouds. The space around the ships is comfortable and inhabitable, and shadows on the water surface and motifs in the background break up the flatness of the sea.

Buttersworth showed little interest in the texture of paint, but his clean and airy palette, delicate tints, sensitive blending, and sure handling allowed him to render precisely the variations of color produced by direct and reflected light rays. Contrasts in the warmth and intensity of hues and the careful juxtaposition of related colors distill mood and give relief to his images. Buttersworth used a bolder palette of elemental colors to convey the hot, dry light of a bright day, when variations flatten out into hues of one color. In his reflective scenes, cool and quiet colors predominate. He highlighted confidently in unsaturated pigment, like the virgin white of his hulls or the rich red of his buoys (plate 26). Buttersworth used a limited number of pigments, but his wide spectrum of high-keyed tones gives diversity to his color scheme. By grading and fusing his halftones and by weighting their warmth and coolness, he could portray half-light and shadow and achieve transparency and luminosity. Tonal harmony unites sea and sky, and the resonance of deep-toned pigments gives coherence to his scenes.

Buttersworth shared many of his techniques with other marine artists. Salmon emphasized clarity and precision, and Bradford and Lane related ships to their environment and explored and extended the limits of seascape. Cozzens captured the essence of yacht racing in watercolor.

What distinguishes Buttersworth from the portraitists and the great majority of American sea painters is his mastery of light and animation. He experimented for years with different renderings of light and reflection until he found his unique formula.[169] Buttersworth had to adjust to the differences in climate and latitude between England and America, where the light is harder and more brilliant and the sky has greater clarity. He was extremely sensitive to light as a medium and adept at indirect lighting. In his *View of Nassau* (plate 46), light strikes the horizon off center, from behind a bank of cloud, and links land, air, water, and shipping. Buttersworth liked to build a unity of effect around a core of distant light that shifts subtly with the clouds. He captured the ephemeral quality and the relative strength of light filtered through limpid air and its shimmering effect when it strikes solid forms or penetrates water. The alternate play of reflected light and shadow on the waves and discreet highlighting give his water a convincing surface. His brightly lit or soft dawn skies with their fresh, transparent air sharpen the contours of his ships and lend them dignity and veracity (plates 6, 23, 25, 26, 40, 41, and 46). Unlike the luminists, whose light is cold, flat, and devoid of life, Buttersworth animated his canvases with diffused warm light.

In contrast to other seascapists, whose works were usually static, Buttersworth also had the knack of conveying the illusion of movement. In his running and storm-tossed seas, invisible gusts of wind or blustering gales are visualized by scudding clouds, rocking buoys, full, fluttering or reefed sails, rippled and choppy water, or mountainous slop splashing over or around the ship. In his narrative action, Buttersworth not only encapsulated the key moment of drama, but implied what came before and what followed. Verve, vitality, and spontaneity make his yachting scenes much more than decorative records of a rich man's sport. His buoyant ships rise and fall in constantly changing seas. His clippers, apart from those modeled specifically for the lithographer, cut through the sea with real momentum and wakes (see page 4). His heeling yachts convey the thrill of speed and sailing under full canvas (plates 25–27, 31, 32, and 34–41).

Buttersworth's style was not painterly or overly self-conscious, and it varied according to subject and mood. It could be both restrained and self-indulgent, prosaic and lyrical, naturalistic and contrived. In many respects, Buttersworth was conservative in technique and firmly rooted in the first half of the nineteenth century, when a form of marine painting was perfected that has never been entirely superseded. He certainly drew on a European tradition and on the linear skills of the portraitist. But he was also an original artist with a virtuoso technique who developed a deceptively simple and distinctive style that strongly influenced his successors. What appears effortless we can in fact assume took him decades to master. His work satisfies as art because it has clarity of form and structure, boldness of design, freshness and immediacy of execution, a true eye for the nuances of opaque and translucent color, and a keen grasp of the properties of light and the laws of motion.

THE ICONOGRAPHY OF MARINE ART

For centuries writers and artists have exploited the allegorical potential of the sea as well as its literal and picturesque qualities.[170] It has been equated with infinity and with the unknowable mysteries of nature. The restless waves have been identified with the vicissitudes of human life, the swings of fortune, and the internal conflicts and external threats faced by society; water has been identified with purity, the lighthouse with hope, and the ship with state and church.[171] As a symbol, the sea has aroused ambivalent attitudes. On the one hand it has been seen as awesome, menacing, wild, uncontrollable, and antagonistic to man; on the other it has appeared alluring, docile, friendly, and a source of life.[172] Until the romantic period, fear of the sea inclined artists to compress it into a window view.[173] Its omnipotence and sudden changes of mood were never really compatible with the serene vision of American transcendentalism. But the ship always had a metaphorical construction in Dutch and Danish painting and was accorded a mystical quality by Caspar David Friedrich.[174]

The rhetoric of any emblematic tradition is ambiguous. It is always difficult to distinguish between the allegorical and the realistic, between poetic and visual imagery, between form and idea.[175] It is tempting for a viewer to read into paintings intentions that exist only in the imagination and are not unequivocally expressed on the canvas. In the search for symbols, the diligent student often displays a more fertile imagination than the artist, and it is often impossible to decide between rival assertions. The eagle that Thomas Cole added to one of his marine scenes could be a nationalist symbol or it could just be a decorative touch.[176] In order to facilitate exposition and reduce the history of art to an orderly progression, artists are often categorized too rigidly into schools, and their work is explained in terminology they would have been unable to understand.[177] In any society, however, traditional precepts and current values, beliefs, and anxieties influence pictorial representation, which is not intended to be a neutral record but to evoke specific emotional responses.

The imagination of American artists was certainly stimulated by the vitality of the sea and its tragic and resonant symbolism. Despite its constant flux, the ocean was both timeless and poignant, and it projected an image of raw beauty and power. If the wilderness was the prime symbol of the American nation, the sea also served as a revelation of God's handiwork and the completeness of creation, and as a retreat from industrialization and cities.[178] Americans were conscious of their maritime heritage before they acquired a sense of national identity.[179] The sea was as important as the wilderness in promoting an expansionist ideology, which regarded the bounty of nature as a justification for materialistic attitudes. The open horizon was both a psychological and an actual frontier, an invitation to self-discovery as well as a means of navigation. Cooper and Melville saw ships as emblems of human passions and attitudes; they linked the sea with adventure, glory, and freedom from the corruption of civil society.[180] The artist Washington Allston employed the ship as a moral metaphor and equated the sea voyage with the voyage of life.

The importance of marine painting as a visual statement of American historical development is beyond dispute. Marine painting celebrated the dominance of the sea in American life before 1860 and glorified the achievements of the captains, whalers, and merchants who had revolutionized transportation and made the fledgling nation rich. Ship paintings are not as reliable and authentic as the architectural drawing, ship model, or physical artifact—a consideration often overlooked by maritime historians—but they provide a record of technological development, the life of the ports, and the routines of seafaring. Precisely because marine art is such a valuable source for nautical history, however, attention has been concentrated on its utilitarian value rather than its artistic quality. Until recently, museums and historians focused on rigging and hull design and the registration and life of ships and neglected the philosophical and cultural aspects of the sea.

It is questionable whether there was ever a unique school of American marine painting or even an indigenous tradition with which individual artists could identify and that was followed with any frequency or consistency. The early Dutch, French, and English schools are immediately recognizable, but by the nineteenth century cross-fertilization among them had reduced their differences. An artistic giant like J. M. W. Turner stands outside any particular tradition. Although marine artists borrowed techniques from the landscapists and were influenced by the revolutions in style that occurred in mainstream art, their genre coalesced around its own special interests and needs. Marine painting was international in character and scope. The sea, and many

of the ships and mariners that sailed on it, had similar features all over the world, unlike the regional topography and inhabitants of landscapes.

In all maritime states, paintings and engravings had long symbolized national strength at sea and served to commemorate naval victories and succor imperialist fantasies.[181] But even European countries with long-standing maritime traditions were slow to recognize their marine artists. The artists had devotees among those who lived by the sea, but they were largely ignored by professional art critics. The taste and possessive instincts of the great art collectors rejected the prosaic and adopted the established canon; marine painting was relegated to the back hall or office or library. Marine artists whose talent could not be denied were simply classified as landscape and genre painters. It was the maritime museums, and not the museums of fine art, that exhibited sea paintings. The same was true of sporting paintings. Racehorses, hunters, and dogs, like ships, were commemorated by their proud owners for their speed and skills and were painted against stereotyped backgrounds. But their portraits were accorded only decorative and documentary importance; George Stubbs's paintings hung unnoticed for generations in the halls of English country houses.[182]

A few critics recognized in the nineteenth century that marine subjects, which overlapped with narrative and genre painting, offered great opportunities to the serious artist. What could be closer to the essential spirit of nature than the sea? Marine art did, of course, have a vocational bias. But if peasants tilling their fields could be accepted as high art, why not mariners fighting wind and wave? The romantic artists were captivated by the passivity and violence, the ebb and flow of the sea, whose solitary grandeur provided an ideal backdrop for narrative painting before it became a subject in its own right. The intrinsic aesthetic qualities of the ship were widely recognized by artists.[183] Ruskin's famous description of a ship as the "loveliest thing ever made" was often cited and was endorsed by the sculptor Horatio Greenough.[184] The drama of conflict between man and the sea was obvious to any traveler. As the famous bully captain of the *Dreadnought* remarked, life at sea had prepared him for anything except Wall Street; his wife reminded visitors to the ship that only six inches of planking "separate us from eternity."[185] Benjamin Champney, the chronicler of the contemporary art world, was shipwrecked off Nova Scotia en route to the salons of Europe and found himself in a lifeboat stuffing a leak with his handkerchief and bailing out water with his hat.[186]

Several factors, however, delayed recognition of the value of marine art. There were too many mediocre and repetitive examples, although portrait and landscape painting also bred a host of amateurs and technicians. Many critics held that no artist could do justice to the sea. Ruskin pronounced it impossible to paint breaking waves, and Stillman declared he had never seen on canvas a storm equivalent to what he experienced at sea.[187] The hierarchical art establishment clung to a rigid and conservative definition of high art. It was hard for ship painters to obtain recognition because they ranked as craftsmen rather than as artists. For centuries ambitious painters had tried to shed their artisan status and differentiate themselves by choosing more dignified subjects. Dependence on commissions and the advent of photography reinforced the old snobbery about painting the commonplace. Jacobsen said that he was "not an artist but a painter of floating property."[188] One art historian suggested that ship portraiture be classified as a separate genre so that it would not undermine the status of marine art.[189]

After the Civil War, America turned its back on the sea and focused on developing the interior. National aspirations were always pulled in contrary directions, toward the ocean or toward the continental landmass. The growth of agriculture and manufacturing in the Middle West created a shift in population distribution, a diversion of energies with corresponding changes in domestic policies. By 1869 both coasts were linked by rail, and California and the West developed their own myths of opportunity. Although the nation's self-confidence rapidly recovered from the agony and disillusionment of the Civil War, the idealistic optimism and heroic spirituality of the earlier period had been dimmed by greater cynicism. By 1876 America was a major industrial power but no longer a maritime power. Although great marine painting does not necessarily coincide with sea power, as is demonstrated by the proliferation of marine painting in France, there certainly was a correlation in Holland and England.[190] In America, too, the decline in maritime power led to indifference: The public no longer wanted to read about young naval lieutenants and pirates or the sea. The new center of gravity was the industrial and agricultural heartland.

These changes were reflected in landscape as well as seascape. The lyrical study of light and descriptive realism became outmoded—the Hudson River school was now regarded as brittle, contrived, empty, unbalanced, and unconvincing.[191] In the 1870s aesthetic criticism was revalued by European academies, which became the major arbiters of style and taste. Americans neglected their native artists, who for inspiration once more turned to European culture, which had a longer tradition and greater sophistication. The Munich and Barbizon schools, British aestheticism, and French Impressionism influenced the new generation of American artists. George Inness, Albert Pinkham Ryder, and Ralph Albert Blakelock rejected fidelity to nature; Winslow Homer and Thomas Eakins embraced heroic realism; and Whistler and John Singer Sargent succumbed to international taste.

The main reason for the dismissive treatment of marine art was its lack of a theoretical base and academic rationale. In a perfect world, artistic talent would be immediately recognized, but in the real world it is subordinate to the whims of fashion; the conformism of an insecure buying public, which defers to experts; the bureaucratic inertia of art institutions; the vagaries of the market; and the marketing ploys of middlemen. Like any professionals, marine artists could acquire intellectual respectability only by developing distinctive and abstruse concepts and a precise technical language to describe and discuss their speciality.[192] Conventional aesthetic theory insisted that taste be disciplined and that art was more than design or a pleasing organization of shapes. Beauty was defined in terms of harmony and symmetrical proportion. What distinguished serious art from the pictorial and the picturesque was its universalism and its synthesis of the real and the ideal.[193] High art had to be permanent, morally uplifting, and capable of intellectual interpretation and justification.

By the nineteenth century landscape painting had finally escaped from exoticism and decorative artifice and had managed to raise itself to the same level as figure painting and human portraiture. It acquired its new status because it was convincingly depicted as an expression of moral virtue, eternal beauty, and the divine order. Concrete ideas were ascribed to the sensory data processed by the imagination of the artist; sublime and pathetic images were presumed to elevate the mind. Even when the highbrow theories associated with the Hudson River school lost their popularity, landscape painting retained its high standing. Painters could enjoy and capture the idyllic splendor of nature without any imperative to seek profound meaning, and many turned to the beach and sea for poetic inspiration.[194] In the twentieth century naive art acquired more than decorative value as soon as new theories were developed that

defended its abstract conceptual design and emphasized its capacity to feel and organize reality without optical fidelity or accurate observation.

Marine painting, on the other hand, was slow to acquire a critical literature of its own or a conceptual structure. Until recently, its audience consisted largely of those who did not belong to the intelligentsia or the art community. Its subject matter provided little opportunity for social interpretation or for the analysis of popular culture, as did narrative and genre painting. Those brought up in an urban or rural environment may also have had greater difficulty relating emotionally to the sea. The technical accomplishments of marine art therefore tended to be overlooked, and it was categorized as functional, documentary, and utilitarian. In some respects, marine painting has benefited from the absence of mannered motifs and a self-conscious ideology. Because it made no pretentious claims, it has been fresher and more innovative.[195] But the price paid has been invisibility in the world of academic art criticism.

Ironically, marine painting benefited from the technological changes that made the sailing ship as redundant as the horse. The ship painting ultimately became a symbol of a defunct era in American history.[196] It seems to be a human

SHIP, SEA & SKY

characteristic to despise technologies when they are dominant and revere them once obsolete. The real cult of sail was
fueled by nostalgia, once technology had eliminated the
risks, inconveniences, and discomforts of sea travel. Each
generation re-creates a mythological past as a counterweight
to unwelcome changes in the present. Time may not, in fact,
be the best critic, because art is either buried indiscriminate-
ly or revived to satisfy a psychological rather than an aesthetic need. The level of appreciation is also determined by
the degree of rarity. Marine paintings have become more de-
sirable as the number of those in circulation has fallen, and
the passage of time has conferred on them the patina of age
and a period flavor.

Buttersworth has long enjoyed a high reputation as
an artist, but the meaning of his paintings has never been
properly explored. There is no sure way of ascertaining what
he hoped to achieve as an artist because he left no written
record of his thoughts. Given his artisan background, lack of
formal education, and exclusion from sophisticated art cir-
cles, he is not likely to have had an aesthetic or metaphysical
theory or an idealistic message like Cole. He does not seem
to have attempted to provide a window into the soul or into
the future. His paintings are ostensibly concerned with factu-

al representation and action, not with profound ideas, emo-
tions, or moral instruction. His style has charm, honesty, and
inspiration but does not revere the past or contemplate the
mysteries of life. His is a reaction to the world through sensibility rather than through ratiocination.

Yet behind every work of art lies a framework of
ideas rooted in contemporary society and culture. Even
when artists are unable to articulate their concepts verbally
or introduce them consciously, the underlying meaning and
significance of their work can still be inferred from the visual evidence of their paintings and is a valid subject for speculation and comment. The content of Buttersworth's paintings reflects both his personal vision of the world and the
influence of that world on him. How did he expect his paintings to be received, and how should they be read?

Buttersworth certainly recognized the intrinsic value
of the particular and emphasized visual certainty. Subject
takes priority over mood. Buttersworth sought to convey the
actual and visible movement, shape, texture, and color of
the sea through blunt, direct, nautical detail. He was not a
full-blown romanticist, as were Birch and Washington Allston in their portraits of ships.[197] Like that of the realists,
Buttersworth's style was anonymous and subordinated to

context; he imposed no obstacles between the viewer and the painting, and he acknowledged the primacy of the individual object. Buttersworth is usually a detached spectator in his paintings, and his paintings describe a definite time and place. He fills them with noisy activity, tension, and nervous excitement. The atmosphere is neither brooding nor poetic, but cheerful and down-to-earth. Occasionally they are subjective in mood, if objective in style. Sometimes he invites the viewer to participate and share his emotional response to nature. The open space and limpid atmosphere of his *View of Nassau* and *Savannah River* (plates 46 and 47) evoke mellow feelings of tranquility and timelessness. Gray clouds and a still sea create a sense of simplicity and intimacy in his port scenes (see page 16 and plate 44). Buttersworth did more than imitate outward appearances or capture transient events. He wanted to evoke the eternal spirit and essential core of nature as manifested in the sea at a particular and tangible moment.

Buttersworth did not populate his seascapes with figures, and the human presence is implicit rather than explicit. Some of his ships are unmanned, even on deck in a storm, and others are driven automatically by wind and wave without any apparent human intervention or intrusion. When crews and spectators do appear, as on the deck of the *Ohio* or in his dories and harbor scenes, they are always small, anonymous, and crowded together.[198] The mariners strain at the ropes with calm self-control, but they are mere instruments of action, neither heroic nor differentiated. The spectators are usually admiring a ship. Buttersworth never personalized his figures in the manner of Homer's fishermen or the inhabitants of contemporary coastal landscapes and beach scenes. He focused on the ship, not on the brutality and risk to life and limb of sailing clippers or the drudgery of three to four years at sea on a whaler.[199] In this respect he did, of course, follow convention, and his customers were interested in the vessel, not in the crew. Buttersworth did not pretend to be a figure painter, and the scale of his figures also had to be proportionate to the size of the ship.

His seascapes are nonetheless comfortable for humans, whose labors are evident even when they are not present. Ships, except in his storm scenes, are depicted within sight of land or other ships or with gulls to indicate the presence of human habitation. Buttersworth also retained some romantic trappings and sentiments, and his inner eye interpreted the character of nature as reassuring. The viewer interacts visually with the natural world from which he is not separated and with which he can identify. Like Lane, Buttersworth relied on the distant contours of shore and ships to shield the tangible volume of his sea space.[200] It is open-ended but not threatening. His seascapes also have an inherently stable equilibrium. Buttersworth never painted passengers cowering in a breaking ship or corpses drifting among wreckage; his shipwreck scenes focus on the rescue, not the disaster (plate 24).[201] He quietly noted the contradictions of human efforts to control the unpredictable forces of nature. But he was always optimistic and emphasized the positive side, the strength and resilience of ships and the courage and willpower of their crews. Buttersworth predicated an orderly and stable environment as manifested by the greater regularity and predictability of maritime transport. Man is not cast adrift in a meaningless void or alienated from nature, which is presented, in the manner of other American landscapists, on an inviting human scale as a coherent, organically ordered, and functional whole.[202]

The relationship between man and nature is symbolized by the ship. Buttersworth's steamers were not intruders on the seas but impressive symbols of the ability of man to control and harness the forces of nature. Buttersworth glorified the sailing ship as an object of grace and dignity in its own right, as a formidable instrument of political power, and as a miracle of technology. His fast clippers and racing yachts exemplify human skill and serve as metaphors for progress through competition. Indeed, the predominant theme in all his work is the symbiosis of ship and sea, which complement and complete each other. The ship visually dominates its setting and remains relatively constant while everything around it is in flux. The ship is more than a human artifact. It is anthropomorphic and functions like the human figures in history painting. Idealized in an organic form, it serves both as the central focus and as a conceptual symbol.

James Buttersworth would have earned recognition had he confined himself to recording fifty years of dramatic developments in the maritime history of America. His prolific output and the broad range of his subject matter have preserved for posterity not only the external appearance of countless ships but the pride and awe they inspired and a unique sensation of how they moved and functioned. But his singular talent raises him above his contemporaries. With an unerring eye, sympathetic instincts, fertile imagination, and refined technique, he experimented in an original way with color and conveyed with unique success the qualities of light and the force of motion. His claim to a place in the canon does not rest only on his documentary importance and efficient execution. Buttersworth achieved the status of a serious artist. He did not confine himself to simple optical realism or to uniform patterns. He was concerned with stating the truth as well as the facts, with the image of the whole painting as well as the image in the painting. His portraits were a means to an end; he moved from the particularity of the ship to the universality of the sea. In his hands, the seascape became a coherent entity capable of provoking an emotional reaction in the viewer. Behind his brush lies a vision of the dynamic interplay and harmony between man and the sea as embodied in the ship. Buttersworth was certainly much more than a painter of the picturesque, and he successfully raised the typical and commonplace to the level of art. His work offers vivid proof that marine painting has a serious content and that it should be regarded as an integral and vital part of American culture.

EARLY PAINTINGS
CLIPPERS AND PACKET SHIPS

EARLY PAINTINGS
(Plates 1–5)

In his early years, Buttersworth borrowed motifs from his father and grandfather and followed the English marine tradition. It is not surprising, therefore, that naval subjects feature prominently among the known paintings of his English period. In the early nineteenth century the ship symbolized national aspirations and political independence. Marine artists were expected by their customers to show the flag and commemorate the ships and battles that had decided supremacy at sea. Although Buttersworth rarely painted actual engagements, he produced many portraits of British, French, and American naval vessels, some of which may have been commissioned by naval officers. He certainly appreciated the importance of naval power. His frigates and ships of the line with their guns run out are depicted realistically as deadly floating batteries, whose enormous firepower would impress and terrify whomever saw them.

CLIPPERS AND PACKET SHIPS
(Plates 6–9)

The elegance of the clippers was largely an accidental consequence of the quest for greater speed, which required a streamlined design. The smooth, curved lines, long and uninterrupted waterlines, and discarded tailboards of the clippers gave them a pristine and uncluttered outline compared with the cumbersome design of their predecessors. They were usually painted black, without exaggerated carved and gilded ornamentation. Their proud figureheads, protruding bowsprits, broad beams, tall raking masts, and long, square-rigged yards with skyscrapers and studding sails exhausted the superlatives of contemporary journalists. Buttersworth is most celebrated for his romantic and poetic images of these greyhounds of the sea, which he did not present abstractly or freeze in a still life. They have beauty in motion and dance to the rhythm of the waves.

1.

Thomas Buttersworth

THE FRIGATE H.M.S. "SEA HORSE" CAPTURING THE FRENCH FRIGATE "LA SENSIBLE"

23 × 35"

From the Collections of the Penobscot Marine Museum, Searsport, Maine

This is a typical scene of a naval engagement by Thomas Buttersworth Senior, who usually emphasized factual details and painted in a stiff formalistic style, employing dark overcast skies, a gray tonality, and muddy, dark green lumpy seas. The warring ships are here modeled smoothly, with clear pictorial definition. The battle is conceived on a grand scale and focuses on the narrative action. H.M.S. *Sea Horse* was a fifth rate with thirty-eight guns, built in 1794 and broken up in 1819.

2.

The U.S.S. "Chesapeake" and H.M.S. "Shannon" in the Battle of Boston

17⅞ × 24⅞"

Collections of McCord Museum of Canadian History, Montreal, Canada (M 402 Painting)

A comparison with plate 1 demonstrates the influence of Thomas on James's early style, when the younger Buttersworth's range of colors was narrower and more monotonous and his palette much cooler. James always retained Thomas's tight draftsmanship, his careful position-ing, and his concern for narrative detail, but in later life his skies became more diverse, his seas more fluid, and his ships more animated. This famous engagement was also recorded by Thomas. The rival frigates were equally matched, the *Chesapeake* having a complement of 379 men and a broadside of 542 pounds compared with 330 men and 550 pounds for the *Shannon*. After taking three broadsides at a range of fifty yards, the *Chesapeake* was boarded and taken.

3.

H.M.S. "Britannia" Flying the Royal Standard

24 × 29"

Private collection

Photograph by Lynton Gardiner

A first rate of 2,616 tons with 120 guns, the *Britannia* was launched in the 1820s, became a training ship in 1859, and was broken up in 1869. Although this painting dates from the 1840s, it was probably intended to represent a visit by the Duchess of Clarence in 1828, since the ship flies the queen's standard. Buttersworth conventionally places the viewer at the waterline and anchors the square composition with a boat with raised oars and a buoy. The influence of Thomas is evident in the fine detail, the use of parallel bands of light to define distance, and the form of the sea. At this time, Buttersworth had still not perfected his technique of illuminating waves, but shadows on the water surface and motifs in the background break up the flatness of the sea. The work is carefully filled by the compact mass of the ships and clouds.

4.

(previous page)
H.M.S. "Rodney" in Plymouth Sound
18 × 24"
Private collection
Photograph courtesy Hirschl & Adler Galleries, Inc., New York, New York

The *Rodney* (206' × 34.5'; 2,598 tons) was built in the 1830s and classed as a second rate with ninety-two guns. In 1860 she was converted to screw propulsion and remained in service until broken up in 1884. The influence of Thomas is apparent in the shadowing of the water, the precise modeling of the *Rodney,* and the sky tones. But the two secondary vessels that provide balance and scale are more characteristic of James, and indeed they both reappear in his later work. As in plate 3, the open foreground is defined by a buoy and bands of light unite the scattered vessels. Buttersworth also manipulated impasto selectively to impart intensity to his brushwork, raising the ship in thicker paint.

5.

A British Frigate Approaching Another Vessel in a Heavy Swell
20 × 24"
Private collection
Photograph by Lynton Gardiner

This frigate may be in pursuit, since both Thomas and James favored chase scenes. A strong English influence is apparent here in the angle of the ship, the arrangement of the waves, and the treatment of the sky. Light from a gap in the clouds strikes the main vessel and leaves the surrounding sea in shadow. The contrast between light and dark color is exaggerated for dramatic effect, and the balance of tension is sustained by vertical and horizontal accents. Buttersworth here echoes Thomas's sense of weather and wind (as in plate 14) and has observed the scene with a polished and selective realism. The composition is further enhanced by imaginative grouping and by turning the axes of the two vessels, which sail diagonally across the waves. The bowsprit of the frigate marks the center of the picture and focuses the action.

6.

(previous page)
THE BALTIMORE CLIPPER "ARCHITECT"
18 × 24"
Private collection
Photograph by Lynton Gardiner

The *Architect* (140' × 30' × 13.6'; 520 tons) was built by L. B. Cully in Baltimore in 1847–1848 for John Ellerton Lodge of Boston and the China trade. The name is suggestive of a break with architectural tradition, and this ship is commonly credited as a prototype of the later and much larger clippers. The firm grasp of linear structure and the optical realism of this painting are reminiscent of architectural drawings. But the painting also depicts the operations of the crew and has a subtly lit sky with variegated clouds and a running sea that opens toward the horizon. Buttersworth reversed the conventional format of dark foreground and light middle ground and created the illusion of distance by the relative scale of secondary vessels and through tonal contrasts. The *Architect* pyramids out, the length of the hull balanced by the verticality of the masts and her rigging and fittings.

7.

SHIP "DREADNOUGHT"
28 × 35"
Peabody Essex Museum, Salem, Massachusetts
Photograph by Mark Sexton

Clipper Ship "Dreadnought" off Sandy Hook. Lithograph, del. C. Parsons pub. N. Currier, signed on the stone by Buttersworth. Peabody Essex Museum, Salem, Massachusetts

Built by Donald McKay at Newburyport in 1853 for David Ogden of New York and the St. George or Red Cross line, the *Dreadnought* (200' × 39' × 26'; 1,414 tons) made seventy-five transatlantic voyages, including a record crossing from Liverpool to Sandy Hook in nineteen days in 1854. She was ultimately wrecked off Cape Horn on July 4, 1869. Buttersworth painted this portrait for the builder, but at least two other versions were completed and were reproduced by Nathaniel Currier. The design of the painting suggests that Buttersworth expected it to be engraved. It is arranged in a network of decoratively balanced patterns, the light sky, highlighted crests, and gulls contrasting with the dark hull and water. The ship dominates the choppy sea and is parallel to a low horizon that is bisected and interrupted by an asymmetrical secondary vessel. The *Dreadnought* is defined against background clouds and sits deep in the water through which it moves with a clear wake. The setting and weather conditions are realistic, with the helmsman and other mariners clearly visible.

8.

(previous page)
THE "CONTEST" AND "YOUNG AMERICA"
22 × 36"
Private collection
Photograph by Lynton Gardiner

Clipper Ship "Contest" and Clipper Ship "Young America." Two lithographs del. F. F. Palmer, pub. N. Currier, 1853, signed on the image by Buttersworth. Museum of the City of New York

Buttersworth here clearly delineates the complex contours of the hulls and rigging, but his canvas appeared too crowded to Currier, who separated and reversed the vessels and reproduced them as two prints. Buttersworth imposed no obstacles between the viewer and the ships and adopted an anonymous approach that subordinated style to content. A light sky and an open foreground is darkened to create depth and because less light is reflected by moving water. A sense of distance is created by gradations of color and tone rather than through linear perspective. The two clippers are lit from behind and fixed in position by two axes of light that run from the foreground to the horizon. Designed by John W. Griffiths and built by William H. Webb of New York in 1853 for George B. Daniels, the *Young America* (243' × 43.2' × 26.9'; 1,961 tons) was heavily sparred, had three decks, and cost $140,000. Employed in the California trade, she made a record voyage from Liverpool to San Francisco in ninety-nine days. In 1860 she was sold to Austria, and she disappeared at sea in 1886.

9.

THE CLIPPER "GREAT REPUBLIC"
17½ × 23½"
Courtesy The Bostonian Society

Launched October 4, 1853, at East Boston, the giant *Great Republic* (325' × 53' × 39'; 4,555 tons) had four masts and decks, an eagle figurehead, and cost $300,000. While at the Dover Street dock on December 26, 1853, a fire spread from shore, and she burned for two days down to the waterline. Her hull was salvaged, and she was rebuilt at a reduced size of 3,357 tons. Sold to England, she eventually foundered in a hurricane off Bermuda in 1872. Buttersworth centers the ship on an axis of two long diagonals, the rounded and curvilinear shape of the hull serving as a counterpoint to the rising points of sails. The vessel is locked into the plane of water by diagonal reflections and by short vertical accents. The structure of the boldly illuminated ship is clarified sharply with a smooth finish, and her sails hang under their own weight and stand out prominently in reverse through careful shadowing. Here Buttersworth models impeccably but he also romanticizes the ship and shows it in the best light.

STEAMSHIPS AND STEAMBOATS
STORM SCENES

STEAMSHIPS AND STEAMBOATS

(Plates 10–13)

Buttersworth recognized and accepted the march of technology and therefore did not confine his attention to sail. He painted a succession of oceanic naval and merchant steamships as well as coastal and river steamboats under a variety of weather conditions. Indeed, he celebrated the introduction of steam propulsion as a heroic as well as a utilitarian innovation. Steamers might have lacked the grace and elegance of sailing craft, but they were impressive examples of human ingenuity and command over the sea.

STORM SCENES

(Plates 14–18)

The hazards of the sea were all too numerous: fog, icebergs, treacherous currents and shoals, reefs and sandbars, hurricanes and typhoons. Their effects could be aggravated by faulty seamanship and by ships that were poorly designed or maintained or overrigged for speed. Buttersworth did not ignore the confrontational aspects of nature, but he resolved this inevitable conflict in a larger unity. He usually depicted ships within sight of land or other ships or with gulls to indicate the presence of human habitation. Although he painted vessels struggling through heavy seas and even a few foundering or wrecked, every dark cloud has a pink lining. Even when his ships are caught by a sudden squall or dismasted by gales, a patch of blue sky suggests hope, and his ships never appear helpless or unable to weather the storm.

10.
THE U.S. MAIL STEAMSHIP "WASHINGTON" FLYING THE MAIL FLAG
PASSING THE "HERMANN" OFF GOVERNORS ISLAND
27¼ × 34¼ "
Mystic Seaport Museum, Inc., Mystic, Connecticut
Photograph by Mary Anne Stets

Built hurriedly in 1847 by Westervelt & Mackey in New York for the Bremen mail route, these were the largest passenger steamers of their day, measuring 230 and 260 feet long, respectively, 39 feet in beam, 31 feet in depth, and weighing 1,640 and 1,750 tons. The *Washington* boasted four decks and an eighty-five-foot grand salon and earned fame by rescuing the passengers of the *Winchester* in 1854 (plate 24). Both ships had checkered histories. They burned too much coal and had difficulty competing with their Cunard rivals. The *Hermann*, originally called *Lafayette*, but renamed to please her German backers, was unstable and underpowered. She was eventually wrecked off Point Kawatzu in Japan in 1869. As in plate 23, the backlighting gives the ship a stark relief, but the scale is drastically diminished in order to accommodate both ships in one picture.

11.

THE STEAM AND SAIL SHIP "WESTERN METROPOLIS"

37 × 52"

South Street Seaport Museum, New York, New York

Photograph by Lynton Gardiner

This side-wheeler with vertical-beam engines (284' × 41' × 23' 3"; 2,269 tons) was built in 1863–1864 by F. D. Tucker of Brooklyn, New York, for L. Brown. She operated both in coastal waters and in the Atlantic and was eventually converted to sail in 1878. This expansive portrait was probably commissioned for a shipping office. The ship is balanced by a lighthouse and a schooner and positioned slightly off center to suggest forward momentum under sail as well as steam. The waves have Buttersworth's characteristic fluidity, with translucent spray thrown up by the bow. The ship is dramatically silhouetted against a cloudbank and a flamboyant sky and is lit from behind by the diffused rays of the sun. The low shoreline and striated clouds empha-size her length, but the horizontality is relieved by the height of the sky.

12.

(previous page)

THE STEAMBOAT "ESCORT" OFF THE BATTERY

20 × 26"

Courtesy The Mariners' Museum, Newport News, Virginia

Built in 1862–1863 by George Greeman & Co. of Mystic, Connecticut, the *Escort* (185' × 28' × 9.6'; 675 tons) was commandeered by the Union in the Civil War and later operated out of Norwich on Long Island Sound. In 1873 she was bought by the Catskill Evening line for Hudson River service, and under Capt. Blanch she served as a mill boat until 1883, when she was rebuilt and renamed *Catskill.* On September 22, 1897, she was rammed by the *St. Johns* near West 34th Street in New York City. Unlike a Bard steamboat, the ship is visibly moving through a real sea. The water is gray green when nearby and gray blue in the distance, where it reflects the sky. The stereotyped topographical details of the shoreline are intended for identification and decorative interest. Buttersworth was careful not to clutter his pictures with superfluous background detail, which might detract from his main subject and cramp his style.

13.

"ARMINA" IN NEW YORK HARBOR

14 × 22"

Private collection

Photograph by Lynton Gardiner

A screw ship (28' × 24' × 3'6"), the *Armina* was built by J. F. Mumm of South Brooklyn, New York, in 1880 and was the flagship of Commodore R.P.H. Abell of the Columbia Yacht Club. The low horizon and deep open foreground place the viewer in close proximity to the steamboat, which moves briskly across the Upper Bay into the wind. Here Buttersworth provides one of his more detailed descriptions of the tip of Manhattan, with close to fifty moored vessels, all depicted with extraordinary clarity. The masts of even the most distant are deftly outlined, and the crew members visible on the decks of the secondary craft demonstrate his gift for miniaturization. The light sky perfectly balances the dark sea. Buttersworth displays his mastery of subtle tonal and color contrasts, flawless shading and highlighting, and an incisive but discreetly applied impasto. He chose a time of day when the sun is low and marked its position with a patch of yellow barely penetrating the cloudbank. The hues of the clouds change imperceptibly from pink and brown to gray and white, until they finally dissolve into a clear blue sky.

14.

Thomas Buttersworth

AN ARMED TOPSAIL SCHOONER IN STORMY WEATHER

17⅞ × 24"

Courtesy The Mariners' Museum, Newport News, Virginia

This typical blustery scene by Thomas illustrates the origins of some of James's mannerisms—
the illumination of the hull, highlighted foam, angle of heel, diffused light, and theatricality
of the break in the clouds. The schooner's rigging and gun decks are depicted with meticulous detail, as are the ships and port in the distance. The canvas is crowded with action, and
a small boat echoes the larger subject. Light and shadow are manipulated to suggest movement through the water, and sharply polarized colors and chiaroscuro define form and generate excitement. Examples like this served as models for the stylized melodrama of James's
storms and cloud formations (plates 15–17).

15.

CLIPPER IN A GALE

16 × 22"

Mystic Seaport Museum, Inc., Mystic, Connecticut

Photograph by Mary Anne Stets

As in plate 16, the ship is probably intended to be the *Young America*. This example well illustrates Buttersworth's ability to convey the effects of weather, the rise of wind, and changes in barometric pressure. The ship buoyantly rides the heavy swell, and a blustery wind is suggested by the mass of rolling water, the scudding clouds, and the fluttering, reduced sails. Despite the turbulence, there is no suggestion of danger, and the ship with its masts pointed toward the sun is in command of the situation. The deck and rigging are spick-and-span, and the crewmen are working with calm purpose. The pattern of clouds sets the mood. As the sky clears, the storm subsides, the sun begins to emerge, and the outer fringes of the clouds turn a delicate pink in contrast to their dark middle tones. Light is cast diagonally over the ship and water and catches the crests of the waves.

16.
(previous page)
THE "YOUNG AMERICA" IN A STORM
12⅛ × 16⅛"
Private collection
Photograph courtesy Hirschl & Adler Galleries, Inc., New York, New York

This is more elaborate and dramatic than plate 15, with the stern almost out of the water, mountainous slop splashing over and around the ship, and no explicit human presence. The dome of black clouds is mirrored by the dark sea at the edges of the foreground. The color balance is faultless, and tonal contrasts separate sky and sea. The power of the wind, the volume of the water, and the sheeting action of waves in sequence are all masterfully conveyed. Here Buttersworth allows his colors to run, and the clouds shift imperceptibly from dark to light gray. He compromises reality in order to produce an attractive picture, since a ship would be invisible in this kind of weather.

17.
THE CLIPPER "FLYING CLOUD" OFF CAPE HORN
20 × 30"
Private collection
Photograph courtesy of collector

Built by Donald McKay in 1851 and sold for $90,000, the *Flying Cloud* (208' × 41' × 21.5'; 1,782 tons) had an innovative hull and rigging and was one of the fastest clippers, twice reaching San Francisco from New York in eighty-nine days. Later sold to foreign owners, she ran aground off New Brunswick and burned while ashore in 1875. The bold, hard silhouette of the ship visually dominates its setting and remains relatively constant while everything around it is in flux. Here Buttersworth shortened the darkened foreground, and neither sea nor sky has clearly defined boundaries. The palpable representation of atmosphere through careful shading and a mixture of hues creates a convincing illusion of pictorial space and helps the narrative. Delicate gray tones tinted with white convey the interaction of light and vapor.

18.
THE CLIPPER "EAGLE" IN A STORM
20 × 30"
South Street Seaport Museum, New York, New York
Photograph by Lynton Gardiner

Built in 1851 by Perry Patterson & Stack of Williamsburg, New York, for Harbeck & Co., the *Eagle* (192' × 38' × 22'; 1,340 tons) was employed in the South American trade until sold to India in 1862. This painting is similar in format to plates 16 and 17. The ship is riding out a storm with only the lower topsails set. Clearly delineated even amid the turmoil, her great size is dwarfed by the immensity of the ocean. She rises buoyantly on the crest of an enormous wave, whose arch is momentarily powerful and hard-edged, the weight of water creating bouncing masses of scattered foam. Here Buttersworth employs chiaroscuro and stark contrasts for visual impact, discreetly illuminating only the crests of the waves, the sails, and the masts. There is no clear division between sea and sky; the ship is centered in a pattern of clouds and waves that merge at the horizon.

MASTERING THE ELEMENTS
YACHTING IN NEW YORK HARBOR

MASTERING THE ELEMENTS

(Plates 19–24)

Shipwreck, collision, and fire were the stock-in-trade of the marine artist. Losses at sea were proportionately more common than modern automobile accidents, and most occurred close to shore; insurance premiums were higher for coastal than for oceanic voyages. Buttersworth recorded several famous disasters and the heroism with which mariners grappled with the violence and unpredictability of the sea. He preferred to emphasize the positive virtues of seamanship and to focus on successful rescue operations rather than on tragedies. The horror is downplayed, and there is no direct appeal for sympathy or consolation for the victims.

YACHTING IN NEW YORK HARBOR

(Plates 25–28)

With their low hulls, schooner rigs, and massive spread of sail in relation to their size, racing yachts offered an impressive profile to the marine artist. Buttersworth almost certainly attended the New York Yacht Club regattas and received commissions from proud owners who wished to commemorate their yachts. In these works he sought to create an impression, not to offer a photographic likeness, and he transformed these records of yachting events into seascapes.

19.

THE "STAGHOUND"

30 × 37"

South Street Seaport Museum, New York, New York

Photograph by Lynton Gardiner

Built in four months by Donald McKay in 1850, with a carved-and-gilded staghound for a figure-head, this ancestor of the extreme clipper (215' × 39'8" × 21'; 1,534 tons) was longer, larger, and more heavily sparred than the earlier packets and was both sharp-bottomed and sharp-ended. She was five feet higher forward than aft, with an elliptical stern, a keel of rock maple and oak, a main-mast of eighty-eight feet, and eight thousand square yards of canvas. Owned by George Upton and Sampson and Tapper, her best run from New York to San Francisco was 107 days. Sold in 1863, she was eventually destroyed by fire off the coast of Brazil. The *Staghound* was unusually un-fortunate with weather. In 1851, she lost her main topmast and three topgallant masts; in 1853 she lost all her sails in a typhoon and drifted for six days. In this study, only the lower topsail, spanker, and staysail are set, and the ship seems to be braced for a storm toward which she is moving.

20.

BRITISH STEAMER "GALLIA"

23¾ × 35½"

Peabody Essex Museum, Salem, Massachusetts

Photograph by Mark Sexton

This is probably a commissioned portrait of the *Gallia* (3,081 tons), which was built at Glasgow in 1879. The lines of the rigging, anchor chain, portholes, ventilation cowls, and stern decoration are all faithfully recorded along with members of the crew, one walking on deck. But Buttersworth has transformed a portrait into a dramatic seascape in which the ship ploughs confidently through a rough sea. The sky forms an arch echoed in the foreground by high waves that anchor the picture. Cloudbanks and another vessel mark off the far horizon. Light is diffused in the sky but concentrated to highlight the wild spray over the bow and deck. Contrasts of light and shadow and tonal variations animate the waves, which change from blue green to green to blue black. Here Buttersworth moves from the particularity of the ship to the universality of the sea.

21.
THE SHIP "UNITED STATES" AGROUND OFF NAVESINK
20 × 27"
Courtesy Maine Maritime Museum, Bath, Maine

22.
THE SHIP "UNITED STATES" WAITING FOR A PILOT BOAT
20 × 27"
Courtesy Maine Maritime Museum, Bath, Maine

Built by John Currier, Jr., of Newburyport in 1866, the *United States* (197' × 20' × 24'; 1,246 tons) was lost when she caught fire at sea in 1876, though the crewmen were rescued. Commissioned by the master to record the successful refloating of his ship, Buttersworth recorded the event in two sequential paintings. In the first, the ship under full sail takes advantage of the tide and the wind. In the second, the lighthouse has changed position and the depth and consistency of the water differ. Sail has been shortened to enter the channel, and the ship is echoed by a pilot boat.

23.

UNIDENTIFIED BRITISH STEAMSHIP RESCUING CREW OF OVERSET SMALL BOAT
13¼ × 17½"
Peabody Essex Museum, Salem, Massachusetts
Photograph by Mark Sexton

The main focus of this restrained but still dramatic picture is the narrative action. Two boats are engaged in the tricky task of picking up two survivors from a capsized sloop, while the crewmen of the side-wheeler watch. In the L-shaped composition, the ship provides the vertical and horizontal lines on one side of the canvas. The stationary steamer is silhouetted against a dark sea and a brightly colored sky, and the sharp contrast adds to the drama.

24.
THE "WASHINGTON" RESCUING THE PASSENGERS AND CREW OF THE "WINCHESTER"
18 × 24"
Private collection
Photograph by Lynton Gardiner

The *Winchester*, a Liverpool packet of 600 tons, set sail on April 9, 1854, with 447 passengers, mainly immigrants. On April 17 she was dismasted and lost her boats in a gale, but she stayed afloat for two weeks through pumping and on April 20 met the *Edward*, which took off fifty passengers. Then she drifted until May 3, when the *Washington* took off the remaining passengers before the ship sank twenty minutes later. Buttersworth was always optimistic in his choice of anecdotal detail, and this scene celebrates the triumph of man over the elements. As the passengers wait hopefully on deck, a small boat bravely challenges the fury of the sea; a gleam of light in the blackness of the storm clouds symbolizes hope.

25.

(previous pages)
"MAGIC" AND "GRACIE" OFF CASTLE GARDEN, NEW YORK, 1871
10¼ × 18⅛"
Private collection
Photograph by Lynton Gardiner

The setting is identified by Castle Garden on the left and Castle Williams on Governors Island on the right. Here Buttersworth uses horizontal bands of light on the water and a diagonal shaft of light from a concealed sun to mark off space and link the competing yachts. The vessels are separated by the water over which they skim but are linked by physical tension, by a shared direction of wind and wave. Visual analogies are provided by highlights of the same pigment. The flags on the ship echo those on the shore, and the colors of the leading yacht echo those of Castle Garden. Different areas of color focus the action. The consistency of the clouds is conveyed by a wash of wet thin paint that was allowed to run, and their mass is suggested by tonal contrasts, which range from pink and orange near the sun to many shades of blue and gray in the storm center and pale blue and yellow in the patch of clear sky. A gradual transition occurs in the water from gray to green and blue tones. Buttersworth used a limited number of pigments, but his wide spectrum of high-keyed tones gives diversity to his color scheme.

26.

"DAUNTLESS" AND "SAPPHO" ROUNDING THE MARK, 1871
13 × 20"
Private collection
Photograph by Lynton Gardiner

This race, in which *Dauntless* beat *Sappho,* occurred in June 1871 at a regatta of the Brooklyn Yacht Club. Built at Mystic, Connecticut, in 1866 by Forsyth & Morgan, the *Dauntless* (123'11" × 25'7" × 9'3"; 268 tons), formerly *L'Hirondelle,* was developed as an ocean racer by Van Devsken and owned by James Gordon Bennett, Jr., between 1867 and 1878. The keel yacht *Sappho* (121' × 27'4" × 12'9"; 310 tons) was modeled by William Townsend and built by C. & R. Poillon in 1867. Originally owned by E. A. Lawrence, she was altered in 1869 and passed to W. P. Douglas. In 1871 she defeated *Cambria* and successfully defended the America's Cup. Here Buttersworth adopts a circular composition, the red buoy and marker acting as a focal point around which the competing yachts turn. The spread sails provide both horizontal and vertical definition and diagonal thrust; the volume of spray indicates the speed of the craft. The fine details of the rigging and the straining crews reinforce the narrative action and suggest the stress imposed on the yachts. The sky is darkened to provide a backdrop, but patches of blue and pink provide relief.

27.

(page 92)

YACHTING RACE IN NEW YORK HARBOR WITH
NAVAL SALUTE AT CASTLE WILLIAMS ON GOVERNORS ISLAND

20⁹⁄₁₆ × 30⁷⁄₁₆"

Museum of Art, Rhode Island School of Design, Providence, Rhode Island

This study of yachts off Governors Island (Castle Williams can be seen on the lower left) offers a vivid example of Buttersworth's use of light to emphasize movement through the water and give coherence to a scene. The sun emerges from a break in the clouds and highlights the huge, wind-stretched sails and the wake of the craft. The sea is a characteristic jade green and is unified in tone with the gray sky. Two American warships in the distance recede diagonally toward the horizon and echo the line of yachts. A horizontal bank of clouds offsets the verticality of the sails. The low foreground and the empty sea with its solitary gull enhance the narrative action. By grading and fusing his halftones, Buttersworth conveyed half-light and shadow and achieved transparency and luminosity.

28.

(page 93)

SCHOONER "RESOLUTE" LEADING THE FLEET AROUND CASTLE GARDEN

22 × 36"

Private collection

Photograph by Joshua Nefsky

Conceived on a grand scale, the *Resolute* (114' × 25'1" × 9'2"; 200 tons), owned by A. S. Hatch, dominates the canvas but is perfectly integrated into the setting. Buttersworth focused the main subject through concentrated lighting and emphasized her intrinsic visual interest through the selection of minute, incidental details. A dark sea and light pinkish sky, shaded at the horizon by a cloud bank, and interrupted glimpses of the shoreline and of other craft, deployed at different angles, accentuate the lines of the schooner and suggest her relative speed. Complementary tones balance sea and sky, and the artist demonstrated his particular skill in depicting the interaction of light and water, both close at hand and in the distance. The strength of the wind is suggested by the tautness of the sails.

AMERICA'S CUP TRIALS AND RACES
FAMOUS YACHTS IN ACTION

AMERICA'S CUP TRIALS AND RACES

(Plates 29–32)

In the nineteenth century, progress was measured by the speed with which packets, clippers, and steamers could cross the Atlantic. The deeply entrenched competitive spirit of *America* fueled a cult of speed. This was nowhere more evident than in international yacht racing. The America's Cup became a focus of patriotic sentiment, and racing became a spectator sport.

FAMOUS YACHTS IN ACTION

(Plates 33–37)

Buttersworth always portrayed ships in an appropriate context and related them to their natural function. Whereas his clippers are majestic and dignified, his yachts have a fragile power and grace of movement at high speed. Buttersworth captured the breathtaking performance of these small craft, the skill and aggressiveness of their hands, the excitement and drama of the race, and the dreams and disappointments of the winners and losers.

29.

(page 96)

THE SLOOP "MARIA" RACING THE SCHOONER YACHT "AMERICA," MAY 1851

15 × 24"

Private collection

Photograph by Joshua Nefsky

The Cutter Yacht "Maria" Racing the Schooner Yacht "America." Lithograph, del. F. F. Palmer, pub. N. Currier, after Buttersworth

The most famous of all yachts, the *America* (87.5' × 22.2' × 9.3' × 11.61'; 146 tons) had a long, low, hollow raking hull, forward-placed masts, and 5,263 square feet of sail. Designed by George Steers and built in 1851, she had a long racing career after her famous victory over the Royal Yacht Squadron in England and survived into the twentieth century, when she was destroyed in a blizzard at Annapolis, Maryland, while awaiting repairs. Originally built as a New York sloop at Hoboken in 1845, the *Maria* (118' × 27' × 8') was altered several times and by 1857 her tonnage had risen from 160 to 216. Designed by Robert Stevens, she had two centerboards, a straight sheer, raking stern, and flaring bow. In this painting Buttersworth depicted the competitors on the same tack and close hauled though traveling in opposite directions. Buttersworth was well aware that the headings of the ships should correspond with the direction of the wind, but he indulged artistic license. When reproduced as a Currier print, the engraver turned the *America* 180 degrees to correct this error and added three men in the cockpit with no wheel. Much is lost in the engraving—the depth of the glazing, the pale lavender and pearl gray overall tone of the sky, and the green gray tones in the sea.

30.

(page 97)

THE FIRST AMERICA'S CUP RACE, AUGUST 8, 1870

22 × 36"

Private collection

Photograph by Lynton Gardiner

This depicts the winning yacht, *Magic,* followed by *Idler* and *Dauntless* rounding Sandy Hook lightship (shown on the far left) in the first race against the English challenger *Cambria* on August 8, 1870. Here Buttersworth outdoes himself in depicting the fast-moving drama of this historic event and demonstrates his fertile imagination, his original use of vibrant color, and his refined technique. The low horizon brings the viewer close to the action, and the billowing sails and storm clouds suggest the power of the wind. Although he usually restrained his colors, here Buttersworth spiked the sky with hotter pigments. The water is a sparkling jade green, and light from a concealed source is sparingly employed with singular effect to highlight the white hull.

31.

THE YACHT "MAGIC" DEFENDING AMERICA'S CUP

29⅞ × 49⅞"

James D. Terra Collection

Courtesy Terra Museum of American Art, Chicago, Illinois. © All Rights Reserved

This is another version of the race depicted in plate 30, though here *Magic* dominates the canvas. The schooner *Magic* (84.6' × 20.1' × 6.0'; 46.77 tons) was formerly the sloop *Madgie,* built in 1856 and lengthened in 1857 by R. F. Loper of Philadelphia. In 1859 she was rigged as a schooner, and in 1869 she was rehabilitated by David Carll of City Island, New York, for Franklin Osgood. Here Buttersworth conveys the thrill of sailing at speed under full canvas and unites subject and mood. As in plate 30, he combines accurate draftsmanship with a strong variegated sky, lively green blue seas, strong contrasts, and fine detail. A bolder palette of elemental colors conveys the hot, dry light of a clear day, when variations flatten out into hues of one color. The brilliant, hard light does not come directly from the sun, but is reflected by the sky. Buttersworth understood well the refractive and reflective properties of light and how it is absorbed.

32.

"MAYFLOWER" LEADING "GALATEA"

25½ × 30½"

Private collection

Photograph by Joshua Nefsky

This depicts the first of a two-race series of the sixth America's Cup challenge on September 7, 1886. The defender and winner, the sloop *Mayflower* (85'6"; 110 tons), was designed by Edward Burgess and built by George Lawley & Son for Gen. Charles J. Paine in 1886; she was later converted to a schooner in 1889. *Galatea* (86'; 158 tons) was designed by J. Beavor Webb for Lt. William Henn in 1885. Although the situation around the lightship may appear a little congested, the steamers carrying spectators did position themselves uncomfortably close to the racing yachts. As a backdrop to the excitement of a close finish, Buttersworth offers one of his spacious and boldly colored skies with subtle combinations of pink and blue and a preponderance of mauve. The force of the wind is apparent in *Galatea*'s sails as her crew bring her round.

33.

"Gracie," "Vision," and "Cornelia" Rounding Sandy Hook
in the New York Yacht Club Regatta of June 11, 1874
26¼ × 36"
Private collection
Photograph by Williamstown Regional Art Conservation Laboratory, Inc.

Here Buttersworth displays his mastery of linear perspective and of all the visual tricks of the marine artist. He creates a visual sense of depth through a progressive diminution in the scale of his vessels. The plane of the water recedes diagonally, and wheeling gulls in the foreground serve as stepping-stones to casually direct the eye outward, not toward a vanishing point in the distance, but along the line of sails and corridor of water in the middle ground toward the lightship. The severity of the infinite horizon is modified by juxtaposing distant ships, including one rounding the lightship, and by the vertical relief of the elongated masts, rigging, and soaring clouds. As on page 1, the leading yacht is shown bow thrusting forward with its crew counterbalancing the wind-filled sails, and its proportions exaggerated to achieve dramatic intensity and a sense of speed.

34.
YACHTING RACE IN NEW YORK HARBOR
(PURITAN LEADING GENESTA)
24½ × 30½"
Private collection
Photograph by Joshua Nefsky

35.
YACHTING RACE IN NEW YORK HARBOR
(PURITAN LEADING GENESTA)
11½ × 17½"
Private collection
Photograph by Lynton Gardiner

These two versions of the same event illustrate how Buttersworth developed his action. Both
are vertical pictures with a dark foreground in which the focus of light is on the leading yacht
approaching a buoy that centers the pyramidal composition. Paddle steamers lined with spectators close the space to the right, and a diagonal line of competing yachts leads the eye to
the horizon on the left. The alternate play of reflected light and shadow on the waves and discreet highlighting give the water a convincing surface. The crewmen are depicted in the hectic
process of adjusting sail in strong wind as the ship turns. In plate 34, however, the viewer is
placed closer to the action, and the vessels and waves have more bulk. The sails are taut, and the
bow throws up spray into the wind as the ship changes direction. In plate 35 the fluttering sails
and the position of the flapping pennant indicate that the maneuver has not yet been completed.

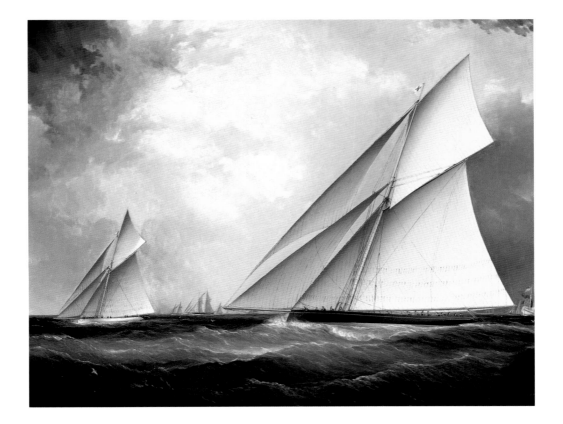

36.
"PURITAN" AND "GENESTA"
23½ × 30"
Private collection
Photograph by Joshua Nefsky

The schooner *Puritan* (81'1" × 22'7" × 8'8"; 105 tons) successfully defended the America's Cup against the challenger *Genesta* in 1885. Originally a sloop, she was built by Edward Burgess for a Boston syndicate headed by General Paine and J. Malcolm Forbes and was lengthened in 1891. In contrast to the traditional wide beam and shallow draft of American centerboard two-masted yachts, she had a cutter rig. *Genesta* (81'7" × 15' × 13'; 80 tons) was designed by J. Beavor Webb and built for Sir Richard Sutton in 1884 and survived until 1900. Here Buttersworth adopts an L-shaped composition, concentrating the action in the middle ground. By placing the long, low hull of *Puritan* parallel to the horizon, Buttersworth focuses attention on the spread of sails, which pyramid toward the sky. By including directly observed details, he captures the tension of the billowing sails, which are echoed by the scudding clouds and by the white crests of foam at the interstices of the waves.

37.
"MADCAP" IN A NEW YORK YACHT CLUB RACE
18 × 24"
Private collection
Photograph courtesy Vose Galleries of Boston

As in plate 34, this crowded canvas has verve, vitality, and spontaneity. It is almost possible to hear the snap of canvas and rope, the groan of the timbers, and the shrieking of the wind through the rigging. In his narrative action, Buttersworth not only encapsulates the key moment of drama, but implies what came before and what follows. The angle of heel is adjusted to display the contours of the yachts more effectively, and the set of sail indicates the strength and direction of the wind. Here Buttersworth displays once more his knack for conveying the illusion of movement. Through subtle nuances of color, the speeding craft appear light and buoyant in relation to the density of the waves, which rise and fall with a fluid actuality.

YACHTS AND OTHER SAILING CRAFT
PORTSCAPES AND SEASCAPES

YACHTS AND OTHER SAILING CRAFT

(Plates 38–43)

The ordinary yachtsman who sailed for recreation, often in sandbaggers and catboats, was excluded from major events by the costs of buying and maintaining a yacht of competitive quality, which also required a professional and highly trained crew. Buttersworth did not, however, confine his attention to one sector of the yachting world, but chose to record a wide variety of craft competing under different weather conditions.

PORTSCAPES AND SEASCAPES

(Plates 44–47)

Buttersworth was not content to imitate outward appearances or to capture transient events. He wanted to evoke the eternal spirit and essential core of nature as manifested in the sea at a particular and tangible moment. He retained some romantic trappings and sentiments, and his inner eye interpreted the character of nature as reassuring. Buttersworth always emphasized the dynamic interplay and harmony of man and the sea. His details are chosen and aligned to emphasize compatibility; his ships blend with one another and with sea and sky. When near the coast or in estuaries, they colonize the expanse of sea; when in the shelter of man-made harbors, they lie peacefully at anchor. Buttersworth relies on the distant contours of shore and ships to shield the tangible volume of his sea space, and his seascapes have an inherent equilibrium. Nature both admits and contains the works of man.

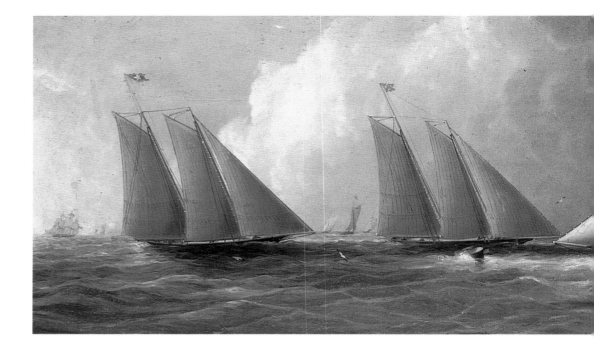

38.

(previous pages)

NEW YORK YACHT CLUB RACE, ABOUT 1850

6¾ × 23¾"

Courtesy New York Yacht Club

Photograph by Mary Anne Stets

This was originally hung on board *Sybil* and depicts that yacht together with *Spray, Cornelia, Ultra* (1848, owner C. B. Miller), and *Una* (1847, owner J. M. Waterbury), a centerboard sloop of forty-six tons built by George Steers. A buoy provides the focal point of the painting, which is illuminated principally by the spray and sails in the right middle ground with a glimpse of the far horizon through a break in the line of ships.

39.

(previous pages)

THRASHING TO WINDWARD

6½ × 25"

Private collection

Photograph by Lynton Gardiner

The vessels form a triangle, and the eye is drawn to the apex at the horizon. The surface likeness of the waves is captured in a broad palette, a mass of dramatically lit foam suggesting the turbulent water. Although not a pair, both pictures were painted for the staterooms of yachts and are similar in size and composition. Their unusual rectangular shape is an extreme example of the horizontal format. In this elongated and circumscribed space Buttersworth is still able to describe the texture of the seamed sails, the speed of the vessels through the water, and the presence of the crews. No vessel moves on the same plane as another, and because they are heeling under the force of wind, the masts can be accommodated within a low framework.

40.

(previous page)

CATBOATS RACING

7½ x 11½"

Private collection

Photograph by Lynton Gardiner

The setting is probably close to New York, since the principal boat is flying the burgee of the Columbia Yacht Club. This painting illustrates perfectly Buttersworth's skill at compressing a complex scene into a small space. The action is centered on a boat pulling away from the foreground, which, to create additional interest, is depicted from the stern. The spacious sky displays a broad range of colors and tones, from the delicate transparent blue of a patch of thin air to a ruddy glow closer to the sun. A black squall on the horizon both frames the boats and suggests the volatile and transitory nature of the weather. The strength and direction of the wind tugging at the sails is indicated by the choppy sea, the fluttering pennants, and the smoke from a steamer. The puffy and frothy clouds have an accurately vaporous and ephemeral texture depending upon their altitude. Horizontal bands of light and the relative scale of the boats create a sense of infinite distance. The sea reflects the sky, and the oscillation of the waves introduces a rhythm and flow that bind together and unify the composition. The lighting is mainly indirect, but the virgin white hull and the red buoy are highlighted clearly in unsaturated pigment.

41.

A RACING YACHT ON THE GREAT SOUTH BAY

9¾ x 11½"

Virginia Museum of Fine Arts, Richmond. Gift of Eugene B. Sydnor, Jr.

This small picture is less crowded with incident and has a quieter, more relaxed mood than other works by Buttersworth. The gleaming hull stands out crisply against a darkening sky and sea, and the taut sails echo the horizon line and catch the fading light from the sun, which is setting behind the clouds. The stillness of the scene and the absorption of the crew convey tranquility and a sense of innocent pleasure.

42.

Four Yachts in a Storm

22 × 36"

Private collection

Photograph courtesy Peabody Essex Museum, Salem, Massachusetts

Photograph by Mark Sexton

Superficially this might appear to be the famous 1866 transatlantic race, but there are four vessels in the painting, and the two most prominent do not match closely any of the three contestants depicted in other paintings of the start of the race by both Cozzens and Buttersworth. Moreover, apart from differences of paintwork, the two yachts in the foreground appear to be identical and seem to represent two different stages of taking in sail. This example represents a transitional stage between the technique of Thomas Buttersworth (see plate 14) and the finished style of plates 16–18. Here James sharply contrasts light and dark, and the light that penetrates the clouds brightens the sea rather than the sky. The arch of black clouds echoes the waves in the abbreviated foreground, and there is no clear horizon. The gray tones of the sky are subtly graded and the gray green sea of the foreground gradually changes to blue in the distance. Despite the turbulence of wind and wave, the ships and their crews taking in sail are clearly delineated.

43.

(previous page)
THE "IRENE," 1854
24 × 30"
Private collection
Photograph by Joshua Nefsky

Three color lithographs of the regatta of the New York Yacht Club, 1854 del. C. Parsons, pub. N. Currier: *The Start*, 17½ × 27½", signed on the image by Buttersworth; *Rounding the South West Spit*, 14⅘ × 28", signed on the image by Buttersworth; *Coming in Round the Stake Boat*, 17½ × 28", after Buttersworth

Here Buttersworth probably painted with an engraving in mind. The uniform sea, the specific draftsmanship, and the sharp contrasts all facilitate black-and-white reproduction. Buttersworth selects dramatic moments that, when presented like still frames in sequence, suggest the course of the whole race. *The Start* provides him with an opportunity to identify the individual yachts before they are seen in action. As in plate 38, he adopts a horizontal format so that he can depict all the competitors moving in the same direction and indicate their relative position and performance. But to break up the monotonous line, he has *Ray* heel over as she comes about and rounds the spit, and he enlivens the action with touches of anecdotal detail.

44.

THE "N. B. PALMER" IN NEW YORK
12 × 16"
Private collection
Photograph by Joshua Nefsky

This may be the picture exhibited at the Art Union in 1853 (# 223) entitled *The Palmer, Clipper, at Anchor*. It serves well to illustrate Buttersworth's tight handling, glazing, and finished technique. The composition suggests both Dutch influence and the work of Robert Salmon. The canvas is filled with details, but the secondary vessels and numerous figures are all clearly delineated, and the horizontal lines of the waves open the picture. Because his brushstrokes were small and unobtrusive, fluid, facile, and unbroken, he was able to execute rapidly with simplicity and directness. To achieve a smooth finish, he thinned his pigments markedly with oil and painted fat and rich with a high degree of saturation proportionate to color. The ground set the overall tonal quality and was allowed to show through in the sky and water. A succession of transparent films of darker pigment was superimposed in thin layers over the lighter underpaint. Cool, quiet colors predominate in this reflective port scene, and the light touch and skillful glazing create an anonymous surface with little texture.

45.

(previous pages)

CHAPMAN DOCK AND OLD BROOKLYN NAVY YARD, EAST RIVER, NEW YORK

8 × 18"

Private collection

Photograph by Joshua Nefsky

Although two versions of this painting survive, this is a rare view by Buttersworth of Greenpoint, Brooklyn. An American man-of-war rides at anchor, and an East River cutter in the foreground flies the pennant of the Brooklyn Yacht Club. As in Buttersworth's views of other ports, such as that of Boston, the shoreline is glimpsed from seaward at a distance, and this is not a detailed topographical study. Buttersworth devoted more space here to the sea, sky, and ships than to the buildings on land. But the evenly spaced waves progress in a repetitive and orderly manner, and the whole scene is suffused with a warm luminosity. The sea space is comfortable for humans, whose labors are evident even though few are present. The viewer interacts visually with the natural world from which he is not separated and with which he can identify.

46.

VIEW OF NASSAU

22 × 30"

Private collection

Photograph by Lynton Gardiner

This is probably the final rendering of a subject that Buttersworth attempted several times; at least one smaller version is known. Here Buttersworth built a unity of effect around a core of distant light; from behind a bank of cloud a shaft of light strikes the inlet at the horizon line off center and links land, air, water, and shipping. His economical and dexterous brushstrokes and his clean and airy palette allow him to render precisely the variations of color produced by direct and reflected light rays. He favored a few dominant, delicately tinted, and sensitively blended colors in reserved hues with little body and carefully controlled modulations of value. The resonance of deep-toned pigments gives coherence to the whole scene, and variations in their intensity re-create the frothy structure of clouds, whose volume is gradually reduced until the sky clears. Careful glazing separates color from form and achieves luminosity and atmospheric depth. In this lyrical painting, subjective in mood if objective in style, Buttersworth invites the viewer to participate and share his emotional response to nature.

47.

THE MOUTH OF THE SAVANNAH RIVER AT COCKSPUR ISLAND

12 × 24"

Collection of Mellon Bank N.A.

Photograph courtesy Mellon Bank Corporation, Pittsburgh, Pennsylvania

In this seascape, the steam paddler and sloop are diminished in scale, but the ships and sea are symbiotically related and complement each other. The open space, brightly lit sky, and limpid atmosphere filled with the weight of humid air evoke a mellow sense of timelessness. Contrasts in the warmth and intensity of the hues and the careful juxtaposition of related colors distill mood and give relief to the images. Nature is here depicted on an inviting human scale as a coherent, organically ordered, and functional entity capable of provoking an emotional response in the viewer.

NOTES

1. Buttersworth's not being literate would certainly explain why, apart from signatures on paintings, no document of any kind written or signed by the artist has come to light. The *Dauntless* drawings of 1851 have captions that resemble the hand of the signature, but they do not appear to have been written at the same time and cannot be ascribed with any certainty to Buttersworth. The majority of American artists did not leave personal archives. See Stebbins, *Life and Works of Martin Johnson Heade*, xiii.

2. Rudolph J. Schaefer, *J. E. Buttersworth, Nineteenth-Century Marine Painter* (Mystic, Conn.: Mystic Seaport Museum, 1975), 16.

3. These included Thomas Cole, Thomas Thompson, Robert Salmon, George Harvey, Robert Havell, Jr., William James Bennett, Thomas Ayres, Thomas Chambers, Edward Moran, George Robert Bonfield, Thomas Birch, the Bards, and George Hayward.

4. Differences in technique and quality between paintings attributed to Thomas also suggest two different artists, though this must remain a hypothesis until the substantial body of work involved has been systematically analyzed. A painting in the City Art Gallery and Museum, Plymouth, England, is signed "T. Buttersworth Snr.," and Hirschl & Adler, Inc., have a record of a night naval action scene signed "T. Buttersworth Jr." A painting of the *Endeavour* off Dover is also said to be signed "T. Buttersworth Jr."

5. One Thomas Buttersworth died in the navy in 1822, and another at St. George's, Southwark, in 1851, but neither seems to have been the marine artist.

6. It is difficult to accept the assumption of Schaefer, *Buttersworth*, 3, that the death certificate should have read seventy-five and not forty-five, and there is insufficient evidence to construct a definitive family pedigree. The International Genealogy Index lists one Thomas Buttersworth whose parents were Thomas and Susanna, but he was baptized in August 1794. Archibald, *Dictionary of Sea Painters*, mentions a painting by Thomas Buttersworth of Queen Victoria's visit to Scotland in 1842, which seems inconsistent with a death date of 1842. But the port background of this painting is identical with a painting of 1827 of the royal yacht at Leith.

7. A copy of the certificate is among the papers of Henry T. Peters and is summarized in Archives of American Art (Microfilm NY 59-19/590).

8. Census Records, Hudson County. The census was officially taken in June 1850, but the ages given for James's children suggest that the return was entered in 1849, and James would have been thirty-one in January 1849. In the 1841 English census James gave his age as twenty-three.

9. Although numerous Buttersworths came into New York in the 1840s (the index to New York landings does not extend beyond 1846) no one can be identified with James. Schaefer, *Buttersworth*, 12, 73, searched the passenger lists of other ports without success. James could, of course, have come by freighter or worked his passage, or he may have been unable to fill out immigration forms. Schaefer suggests that he must have been in New York by 1847 since a Currier print that year, *Ship of the Line in a Gale*, resembles a painting by James. But there are too many differences between the print and the painting, and many similar compositions exist.

10. Doggett's New York City Directory, 1849–50; this is the only year for which he is listed.

11. Stanley C. Johnson, *A History of Emigration from the United Kingdom to North America, 1763–1912* (London: G. Routledge & Sons, 1913), App. 1; Ira Rosenwaike, *Population History of New York City* (Syracuse, N.Y.: Syracuse University Press, 1972), Table 9; Charlotte Erickson, *Invisible Immigrants* (London: Weidenfeld and Nicolson, 1972), 16; Albion, *Rise of New York Port*, Apps. 27–28.

12. *The British Mechanic's and Labourer's Handbook and True Guide to the United States with Ample Notices Respecting Various Trades and Professions* (London: Charles Knight and Co.), 206, 238–42.

13. Schaefer, *Buttersworth*, 76–80. There were numerous other sources for painting the race, like the sketch from life by Oswald W. N. Brierly and the version by Charles Sargent, both reproduced in Thompson et al., *The America*, 108. If James did visit England, it must have been for urgent personal reasons or in response to a commission to paint the English yachts.

14. A. Blaugrund, "The Tenth Street Studio Building," *American Art Journal* 14 (1982): 66.

15. Robert R. Stinson, *Hudson County Today* (Union, N.J.: *Hudson Dispatch*, 1915), 34. A view of Hoboken circa 1852 by John Bornet is illustrated in Koke, ed., *American Landscape and Genre Paintings in the New-York Historical Society*.

16. Hudson County Deed Book 14, 569. The lots were #9–10, 83–84. Lot 9 was on block #20 and bounded by West Street in the front and Derotta Lane in the rear, twenty-five feet front and rear and one hundred feet deep. Lot 84, on the southern side of which stood the house, was the same size and one hundred feet from Paterson Avenue. Lots 10 and 83 were sold on April 30, 1870, for $4,000.

17. Hudson County Deeds 21:52; 202:67; 205:191; 218:50; her will is dated August 21, 1883. The lot numbers were 4, 5, and 18, and some were sold during her lifetime. She also had an account with the Bowery Savings Bank. When she died in 1919, the daughter, Ann, bequeathed by will $3,500 in real estate and $1,011.87 in cash.

18. Among the Schaefer papers is a photograph of the house owned by James, Jr.

19. A painting by Buttersworth of the Graff house at Pleasant Plaine, entitled *The Homestead*, is illustrated in Schaefer, *Buttersworth*, plate 11.

20. Hudson County Surrogates Court (14549). The fates of his sons William (born 1843) and Edward (born 1845) are unknown.

21. Hudson County Surrogates Court (14549); Administration Papers of the Estate of James Edward Buttersworth. It took his son only eleven days after his father's death to draw up the inventory of his estate.

22. Albion, *Rise of New York Port*, 18, Apps. 2 and 11; Albion, Baker, and Labaree, *New England and the Sea*, 99.

23. Two examples are a watercolor by John Henry Hill of the East River in 1852 illustrated in Koke, ed., *American Landscape and Genre Painting*, I, No. 1218, and an aerial view of the

tip of Manhattan in a Currier & Ives lithograph of 1872.

24. H. J. Smith, *Romance of the Hoboken Ferry* (New York, 1931). For a map of the streets and ferries, see Johnson and Lightfoot, *Maritime New York in Nineteenth-Century Photographs.*

25. Robert Greenhalgh Albion, *Square-Riggers on Schedule: The New York Sailing Packets to England, France, and the Cotton Ports* (Hamden, Conn.: Archon Books, 1938), 81.

26. Mckay, *Some Famous Sailing Ships,* chap. 22. For record passages, see Clark, *The Clipper Ship Era,* App. 2. Their fast runs were aided by M. F. Maury's famous *Sailing Directions,* which analyzed the direction of winds and currents from navigational data.

27. On differences between American and English clippers, see David R. McGregor, *Fast Sailing Ships, Their Design and Construction, 1775–1875* (Switzerland: EDITA, 1973), 186–87.

28. J. L. Stakesbury, "The King of the Clipper," *American History Illustrated* 6 (1972): 4–9.

29. Loading and size as well as design affected speed. Howard Irving Chapelle, *The Search for Speed under Sail, 1700–1855* (New York: W. W. Norton, 1967), discusses design and rigging.

30. Schaefer, *Butterworth,* plate 5; Chapelle, *The Baltimore Clipper,* 145.

31. Fairburn, *Merchant Sail,* III, 1,601; V, 2, 947–48.

32. Albion, *Square-Riggers,* 98, 202.

33. A map of the areas served by steamboats is printed in Carl D. Lane, *American Paddle Steamboats* (New York: Coward McCann, 1943), 16.

34. Dayton, *Steamboat Days,* ix.

35. For an excellent account of the harsh realities of early steamship travel, see E. W. Sloan in *The Atlantic World of Robert G. Albion,* ed. Benjamin W. Labaree (Middletown, Conn.: Wesleyan University Press, 1975), chap. 5; Ridgely-Nevitt, *American Steamships on the Atlantic,* 187–88.

36. Morrison, *History of the New York Ship Yards,* 89. A painting by Pringle of the Smith and Simon Shipyard at Fourth Street is printed in Richard C. Mckay, *South Street: A Maritime History of New York* (New York: G. P. Putnam's Sons, 1934), 187, and also a pencil sketch of a figurehead-carver's shop, 400.

37. Edwin L. Dunbaugh and William du Barry Thomas, *William H. Webb: Shipbuilder* (Glen Cove, N.Y.: Webb Institute of Naval Architecture, 1989), 38; Fairburn, *Merchant Sail,* V, chap. 3; Albion, *Rise of New York Port,* chap. 14.

38. On the Maine yards, see Baker, *Maritime History of Bath, Maine.*

39. John Robinson and George F. Dow, *The Sailing Ships of New England,* series 2 (Salem, Mass.: Marine Research Society, 1924), 34.

40. Miller, *The New York Coast-Wise Trade.*

41. Bauer, *Maritime History of the United States.*

42. Morrison, *History of American Steam Navigation,* 412; Tyler, *Steam Conquers the Atlantic,* chaps. 10–15.

43. Ridgely-Nevitt, *American Steamships on the Atlantic,* chaps. 7, 10.

44. *The Evening News* (Hoboken, N.J., 1893).

45. John Parkinson, *History of the New York Yacht Club from Its Founding through 1973* (New York: The Club, 1975), 6, 7.

46. Alfred F. Loomis, *Ocean Racing: The Great Blue-Water Yacht Races, 1866–1935* (New York: William Morrow and Co., 1936), chap. 1; Stephens, *Traditions and Memories of American Yachting,* 14.

47. Rousmaniere, *Golden Pastime,* 122.

48. Chapelle, *History of American Sailing Ships,* 174, 313.

49. Rousmaniere, *Golden Pastime,* 46.

50. Thompson and Swan, *The Yacht America,* passim. For subsequent changes in the course and rules, see Rayner, *Winning Moment,* and Lester and Sleeman, *America's Cup, 1851–1987.*

51. *George Robert Bonfield,* Introduction.

52. Roger B. Stein, *John Ruskin and Aesthetic Thought in America, 1840–1900* (Cambridge, Mass.: Harvard University Press, 1967), 11, 21.

53. Russel Blaine Nye, *Society and Culture in America, 1830–1860* (New York: Harper & Row, 1974), 186; Flexner, *That Wilder Image,* 106–109.

54. Lillian B. Miller, *Patrons and Patriotism: The Encouragement of the Fine Arts in the United States, 1790–1860* (Chicago: University of Chicago Press, 1966), 170, 228.

55. Lois Marie Fink and Joshua C. Taylor, *Academy: The Academic Tradition in American Art* (Washington, D.C.: Smithsonian Institution Press, 1975), 69.

56. Richardson, *Painting in America,* 214.

57. Richardson, *American Romantic Painting,* 21.

58. K. J. Avery in *American Paradise, The World of the Hudson River School,* ed. John K. Howat (New York: Metropolitan Museum of Art, 1987), note 96.

59. Neil Harris, *The Artist in American Society, the Formative Years, 1790–1860* (New York: George Braziller, 1961), 58–64, 262–68.

60. Howat in *American Paradise,* 61ff.

61. Johnson and Lightfoot, *Maritime New York.*

62. "Dollars and Cents of Art," 30.

63. Wilmerding, *Robert Salmon,* 73.

64. Stebbins, *Heade,* 4.

65. Harry Twyford Peters, *America on Stone: The Other Printmakers to the American People* (Garden City, N.Y.: Doubleday, Doran and Co., 1929), 261.

66. Benjamin Champney, *Sixty Years' Memories of Art and Artists* (Woburn, Mass.: Wallace & Andrews, 1900), 20; Ferber, *William Trost Richards,* 14.

67. Kelley, *American Yachts,* contains both outline drawings and a portfolio of excellent prints of watercolor studies by Cozzens, which are also reproduced in Ahmed John Kenealy, *Yacht Races for the America's Cup, 1851–1893* (New York: Outing Co., 1894). Cozzens's approach to yachting was cooler and less dramatic than James's. There are numerous paintings and prints of yachting scenes by obscure artists.

68. Howland, "A. Cary Smith," 65.

69. *The Autobiography of Worthington Whittredge,* ed. J. I. H. Baur, *The Brooklyn Museum Journal* 1 (1942): 10.

70. *Ex-voto marins de Méditerranée,* ed. Jean Lepage and Eric Rieth (Paris: Le Musée de la Marine, 1978), 18.

71. The *Washington* was, for example, also painted by German artists: see Frank O. Braynard, "A Tale of Two Pictures," *American Neptune* 27 (October 1967): 255; Smith, *The Artful Roux.*

72. These figures have been roughly calculated from Brewington, *Dictionary of Marine Artists,* after excluding the most ephemeral.

73. Pisano, *Long Island Landscape Painting,* 21–22; *Maine and Its Role in American Art,* ed. G. A. Mellor and E. T. Wilden (New York, 1963), 84. Examples would include William M. Davis, I. R. Wiles, C. J. Waldron, Charles Torrey, I. R. Hughes, S. J. Cresey, and Franklin Stanwood.

74. Peluso, "Life and Work of Jacobsen," 66.

75. Peluso, "The Hoboken School," passim.

76. Wilmerding, *American Marine Painting,* 59. One example is illustrated by J. I. H. Baur,

"The U.S. Faces the Sea," *Art News* 47 (1948): 22.

77. This is illustrated in Robinson and Dow, *Sailing Ships of New England*. Many portraits survived in the hands of families of the original builders.

78. Archives of American Art, Roll 511, papers of F. W. Robinson; *Five Centuries of Marine Painting* (Exhibition Catalogue, Detroit Institute of Arts, 1942), 33.

79. Catalogue of Sale at Plaza Galleries, February 1, 1945.

80. Peter C. Marzio, *The Democratic Art: An Exhibition on the History of Chromolithography in America* (Fort Worth, Tex.: Amon Carter Museum of Western Art), 90, 97.

81. *Currier & Ives, A Catalogue Raisonné*, lists only ten prints.

82. Schaefer, *Buttersworth*, 14. Alice Jacobi recalled in an interview with Schaefer that Buttersworth would visit galleries in New York where his paintings were displayed.

83. Clark S. Marlor, *A History of the Brooklyn Art Association with an Index of Exhibitions* (New York: J. F. Carr, 1970); Marie Naylor, *The National Academy of Design Exhibition Record, 1861–1900* (New York: Kennedy Galleries, 1973); Eliot Candee Clark, *History of the National Academy of Design, 1825–1953* (New York: Columbia University Press, 1954); *Report of the International Maritime Exhibition 1889–90*, ed. J. W. Rychkman (Boston, 1890). Among the painters exhibited at the latter were FitzHugh Lane, Stubbs, Thomas Eakins, W. T. Richards, Bradford, Winslow Homer, W. E. Norton, Clement Drew, J. G. Tyler, Edward Gay, and De Haas. A search through exhibition catalogues of the period has produced no examples of Buttersworths, though, of course, many catalogues have not survived.

84. Jacobsen, *Frederick Cozzens*, 200.

85. "Dollars and Cents of Art," 30.

86. Stebbins, *Heade*, 41–42.

87. Wilmerding, *American Marine Painting*, 134.

88. Jacobsen, *From Sail to Steam*, 19.

89. Wilmerding, *Robert Salmon*, xv–xvi, 32.

90. *Report of International Maritime Exhibition*, 102. In comparison, William Bradford was priced at $450, W. T. Richards at $350–800, Winslow Homer at $100 for a watercolor, Thomas Eakins at $150–250, and Cropsey at $50–150.

91. Beam, *Winslow Homer at Prout's Neck*, 82. Artists often adopted eccentric attitudes to pricing. Homer discouraged Lawson Valentine from buying his *Breezing Up*, as he thought the quality did not justify a price of $850; see John Wilmerding, Linda Ayres et al., *Winslow Homer in the 1870s: Selections from the Valentine-Pulsifer Collection* (Princeton: The Art Museum, Princeton University, 1990), 44.

92. Mary Bartlett Cowdrey, *American Academy of Fine Arts and American Art Union, 1816–52* (New York: The New-York Historical Society, 1953).

93. The cost of paints is difficult to estimate, though it must have been considerable. Some prices are given in *Devoe and Raynolds Co. Priced Catalog of Artists' Materials* (New York: F. W. Devoe & Co., 1878).

94. Stebbins, *Heade*, 41, 173.

95. Ralph Andreano, "Trends and Variations in Economic Welfare," in *New Views on American Economic Development, A Selective Anthology of Recent Work*, ed. Ralph Andreano (Cambridge, Mass.: Schenkman Publishing, 1965), 153; Edgar Martin, *The Standard of Living in 1860* (Chicago: University of Chicago Press, 1942), 393, chap. 6; John Rogers Commons, *History of Labour in the United States* (New York: Macmillan, 1918), I, 487; Clarence Dickinson Long, *Wages and Earnings in the United States, 1860–1890* (Princeton, N.J.: Princeton University Press, 1960). Only 1 percent of the population earned more than $842 per annum, and as late as 1870 a town laborer earned only $1.55 a day without board.

96. D. Brady, "Relative Prices in the Nineteenth Century," *Journal of Economic History* 24 (1964): 184.

97. *The British Mechanic's Handbook*, 207, 235.

98. The fundamental catalogue raisonné is that of Schaefer, *Buttersworth*, who lists 548 paintings, 18 pencil and wash drawings, and 143 possibles. The 1992 tally of the Smithsonian Institution, National Collection of Fine Art Inventory of American Paintings and Artists Names, is 879 as well as 5 Buttersworths and 1 A. H. Buttersworth. Even Schaefer had to rely in part on photographs, and many items listed in the Smithsonian inventory are not based on a critical examination of actual paintings. There are undoubtedly some duplicates and misattributions; the same painting of H.M.S. *Trafalgar* occurs more than once, and both sales and resales are listed as well as present ownership. Any total must be approximate, because new examples constantly surface and then disappear in the market. Frequently paintings are identified only by ambiguous titles, and there is a danger of double-counting. It can nevertheless be safely presumed that known examples represent no more than half of James's output.

99. Wilmerding, *Robert Salmon*, xi; Stebbins, *Heade*, estimates that 50 to 75 percent of Heade's paintings have disappeared.

100. Brook-Hart, *British Nineteenth-Century Marine Painting*, plate 12, illustrates the *Victory*. A battleship, 30" × 50", and H.M.S. *Collingwood* are on loan to the Department of State. Many other examples are listed by Schaefer, *Buttersworth*, and by the Smithsonian.

101. Schaefer, *Buttersworth*, 202.

102. A portrait of the *Atlantic* passed through Vose Galleries, Boston.

103. These are listed in the Smithsonian inventory in addition to those in Schaefer, *Buttersworth*. In many cases their authenticity cannot be verified.

104. Schaefer, *Buttersworth*, 118–19. Unlike some artists, James seems to have signed as a matter of course, though he must have sometimes worked on commission for patrons who preferred that the artist remain anonymous.

105. A batch of paintings signed J. E. Buttersworth, including several landscapes, were originally owned by the Morris family of Staten Island, and it is conceivable that these descended from Ann Buttersworth Graff. Schaefer, *Buttersworth*, 220, also suggests that certain design features introduced after 1894 occur in some yacht paintings.

106. The son's signature on the documents winding up his father's estate closely resembles that on the paintings.

107. Henry Theodore Tuckerman, *Book of the Artists* (New York: G. P. Putnam & Son, 1867), 27.

108. No canvases have been subjected to X-ray examination or chemical analysis of the paint, as most had to be viewed under conditions that precluded a systematic technical examination. It has, however, been possible to inspect a few damaged paintings where the canvas has been exposed. Conservation records have also been consulted where available, and information has been received from restorers who have worked on James's paintings. So small a sample of canvases may not be typical, and the remarks that follow should not be regarded as conclusive.

109. Cordingly, *Painters of the Sea*, Introduction.

110. Two typical examples are illustrated by Schaefer, *Buttersworth*, plates 14 and 24.

111. Wilmerding, *American Marine Painting*, 146.

112. This is evident from a comparison of three paintings of a stern chase illustrated in *Concise Catalogue of Oil Paintings in the National Maritime Museum* (Woodbridge, Suffolk: Antique Collectors' Club, 1988). Another example is in the Atwater Museum, Philadelphia.

113. On the extraordinary quality and range of Dutch engravings and paintings, see Irene de Groot, *Maritime Prints by the Dutch Masters* (London: Gordon Fraser, 1980), and *Eloge de la navigation hollandaise au XVIIe siècle* (Paris: Fondation Custodia, 1989).

114. Wilmerding, *Robert Salmon*, 62–63.

115. G. S. Keyes, *Mirror of Empire. Dutch Marine Art of the Seventeenth Century* (New York:

Cambridge University Press, 1990), 26, 55–57.

116. T. S. R. Boase, "Shipwreck in English Romantic Painting," *Journal of the Warburg and Courtauld Institutes* 22 (1959): 333.

117. Cordingly, *Marine Painting in England*, 72.

118. Linda S. Ferber and William H. Gerdts, curators, *The New Path: Ruskin and the American Pre-Raphaelites* (Brooklyn, N.Y.: The Brooklyn Museum; Schocken Books, 1985), 113, 131; R. Stein, *John Ruskin and Aesthetic Thought* (Cambridge, Mass., 1987), 103; Allen Staley, *The Pre-Raphaelite Landscape* (Oxford: Clarendon Press, 1973), 185.

119. Stebbins, *Heade*, 106.

120. Wilmerding, *American Light*, 33.

121. *Jasper F. Cropsey, 1823–1900: A Retrospective View of America's Painter of Autumns*, ed. Peter Bermingham (College Park: University of Maryland, 1968).

122. Schaefer, *Buttersworth*, 44.

123. *American Paradise*, 32.

124. Ila S. Weiss, *Poetic Landscape: The Art and Experience of Sanford R. Gifford* (Newark, Del.: University of Delaware Press, 1987), 317; John Paul Driscoll et al., *John Frederick Kensett, An American Master* (New York: Worcester Art Museum, 1985), 53.

125. Baker, "Elisha Taylor Baker."

126. Interview with Alphonse Jacobsen, summarized in Whitmore, "Jacobsen"; Peluso, *J. & J. Bard*, 17.

127. William H. Gerdts, *Painting and Sculpture in New Jersey* (Princeton, N.J.: Van Nostrand, 1964), 121.

128. Peluso, "The Hoboken School," passim.

129. A painting of the *Narragansett* passed through Hirschl & Adler, New York.

130. Novak, *American Painting of the Nineteenth Century*, 98.

131. Wilmerding, *FitzHugh Lane*, 34, 83.

132. Wilmerding, *American Marine Painting*, 146.

133. The two portraits illustrated in Schaefer, *Buttersworth*, 187, appear to be copies and may well have been painted by his son.

134. A painting of the *Constitution* firing on a French privateer, 8" × 10", passed through Vose Galleries, Boston.

135. Schaefer, *Buttersworth*, 78.

136. Brown, *Alfred Thomas Bricher*.

137. Schaefer, *Buttersworth*, 120, plate 10.

138. An unsigned watercolor of H.M.S. *Chesapeake* is at Mystic Seaport Museum, Mystic, Connecticut.

139. Schaefer, *Buttersworth*, plate 16.

140. In two examples in the Penobscot Museum there is a visible line across the canvas.

141. They are illustrated by Schaefer, *Buttersworth*, 76–80.

142. Ibid., illustrations 61–62.

143. Ibid., illustrations 65, 124, 141, 153.

144. The other version of the *Flying Cloud* is reproduced in color from a private collection on the dust jacket of A. B. C. Whipple, *The Challenge* (New York: William Morrow and Co., 1987).

145. A set of Gibraltar scenes is in the Penobscot Museum, and there were clearly others. A storm off Gibraltar, 15" × 23", with a black sky and lightning flashes, passed through

Hirschl & Adler, New York.

146. There are, for example, two signed and one unsigned versions of the action between the *President* and the *Endymion* in the New-York Historical Society and the Penobscot Museum as well as an aquatint by Joseph Jeake.

147. Wilmerding, *FitzHugh Lane*, 62, 66.

148. Legend also records that in 1854 James Hamilton insisted he be lashed to a mast in a storm; see Arlene Jacobowitz, *James Hamilton, 1819–1878, American Marine Painter* (Brooklyn, N.Y.: Brooklyn Museum, 1966), 14. The story about Vernet was circulated later to grant him the status of a romantic hero; see G. Levitine, "Vernet Tied to a Mast," *The Art Bulletin* 49 (1967):100; Ferber, *William Trost Richards*, 30.

149. Sidney Bressler, *Reynolds Beal, Impressionist Landscapes and Seascapes* (Rutherford, N.J.: Fairleigh Dickinson University Press, 1989), 44.

150. The importance of visual memory was stressed by many marine artists: see, for example, Waugh's comments on technique in G. R. Havens, *Frederick J. Waugh* (University of Maine Studies 89, 1969), 214.

151. Schaefer, *Buttersworth*, 155.

152. Elizabeth Lindquist-Cock, *The Influence of Photography on American Landscape Painting, 1839–1880* (New York: Garland Publishing, 1977), vii.

153. For an example, see Schaefer, *Buttersworth*, 139.

154. *American Marine Painting; A Loan Exhibition on Display at Virginia Museum; Realism and Romanticism in Nineteenth-Century New England Landscape*, 4; Wilmerding, *FitzHugh Lane*, 47. Van Beest did a preliminary watercolor drawing, and Lane painted the scene in reverse composition.

155. Lane Fine Art of London, in 1987, advertised a pair of naval scenes off Gibraltar, dated 1846.

156. Schaefer, *Buttersworth*, 23.

157. Examples would include his *Phoenix* of Baltimore and several of his Mediterranean and South American subjects; see Schaefer, *Buttersworth*, illustration, 46.

158. Gombrich, *Art and Illusion*, xiii.

159. *Reflections of an Era*, Introduction.

160. Schaefer, *Buttersworth*, 47, 144.

161. Ibid., 45.

162. Ibid., 51.

163. Ibid., 62, plate 2.

164. Ibid., plate 14.

165. Ibid., illustrations 197–98.

166. On the differences, see Dunning, *Changing Images of Pictorial Space*, 44.

167. Schaefer, *Buttersworth*, illustrations 179, 192.

168. Ibid., plate 19.

169. One example of an unsuccessful attempt is the *Valparaiso* illustrated in Schaefer, *Buttersworth*, 123.

170. Goedde, *Tempest and Shipwreck*, Introduction.

171. W. H. Auden, *The Enchafed Flood; or, The Romantic Iconography of the Sea* (New York: Random House, 1950), 8; Margarita Russell, *Visions of the Sea: Hendrick C. Vroom and the Origins of Dutch Marine Painting* (Leiden: published for the Sir Thomas Browne Institute by E. J. Brill and Leiden University Press, 1983), 71–78.

172. Downes, "American Painters of the Sea," 301; G. Eager, "The Iconography of the

Boat," *Art Journal* 35 (1976): 224; J. Schrier, "Art Symbols and the Unconscious," *Journal of Aesthetics and Art Criticism* 12 (1953): 68–72.

173. Stein, *Seascape and Imagination*, 31.

174. Henrick Boe Bramsen, *Danish Marine Painters*, translated from the Danish by David Hohnen (Copenhagen: Burmeister & Wain, 1962), 36.

175. Eitner, "The Open Window and the Storm-Tossed Boat," 290.

176. Parry, *Art of Thomas Cole*, 305.

177. Wilton, "American Light," 715.

178. Baigell, *Thomas Cole*, 10.

179. Wilmerding, *American Marine Painting*, 9.

180. Philbrick, *James Fenimore Cooper and the Development of American Sea Fiction*, 261–65.

181. Compare Wilmerding, *American Marine Painting*, with Cordingly, *Painters of the Sea*, 28.

182. J. Basker, "George Stubbs," in John Wilmerding, ed., *Essays in Honor of Paul Mellon, Collector and Benefactor* (Hanover, N.H.: University Press of New England, 1986), 33.

183. Stein, *Seascape and the American Imagination*, 63.

184. New-York Historical Society, Microfilm 46, Diary of Miller, April 1, 1850; *The Crayon* in April 1856 quoted Ruskin and noted the launch of the *Niagara* at the New York Navy Yard; Stein, *Seascape and Imagination*, 63; S. Crane, "The Aesthetics of Horatio Greenough in Perspective," *Journal of Aesthetics and Art Criticism* 24 (1966): 420.

185. Samuel Samuels, *From the Forecastle to the Cabin* (Boston: C. E. Lauriat Co., 1924), 255.

186. Champney, *Sixty Years' Memories*, 81.

187. Roger Quarm in Scott Wilcox, *Masters of the Sea: British Marine Watercolours* (Oxford: Phaidon Press, 1987), 64; John Ruskin, *Modern Painters* (New York: H. M. Caldwell,

1856–59), vol. 2, 368; William James Stillman, *The Autobiography of a Journalist* (Boston: Houghton Mifflin & Co, 1901), 294–96.

188. Whitmore, "Jacobsen."

189. Boye Meyer-Friese, *Marinemalerei in Deutschland im 19. Jahrhundert* (Oldenburg: Stalling, 1981).

190. Wilmerding, *American Marine Painting*, 67.

191. Stebbins, *Heade*, 96.

192. Fink and Taylor, *Academy*, 12, argue that a common language was needed that was intelligible to all, though, of course, a major objective of such a language is to exclude outsiders.

193. Novak, "Basic Aesthetic Guidelines," 88.

194. Berko and Berko, *Seascapes of Belgian Painters*, Introduction.

195. Wilmerding, *American Marine Painting*, Preface.

196. Although it is doubtful whether the steam locomotive and truck have generated a body of painting on the scale and quality of the ship portrait, the airplane may prove to be a twentieth-century equivalent.

197. Wilmerding, *American Marine Painting*, 83.

198. Schaefer, *Buttersworth*, illustration, 95.

199. Morison, *Maritime History of Massachusetts*, 323.

200. Nelson, *Sounding the Depths*, 24.

201. A particular example is plate 24.

202. Wilmerding in *The Eden of America, Rhode Island Landscapes*.

SUGGESTIONS FOR FURTHER READING

Those seeking a comprehensive guide to the vast literature on maritime history should consult Robert Greenhalgh, *Naval & Maritime History; An Annotated Bibliography* (4th ed., Mystic, Conn.: Marine Historical Association, 1972) and Susan K. Kinnell, *American Maritime History, A Bibliography* (Santa Barbara: ABC-CLIO, 1986). Attention has been focused here on the relatively few works related specifically to American marine art of the nineteenth century.

CATALOGUES RAISONNES AND COLLECTIONS
"Antonio Jacobsen, Steamship Paintings." *American Neptune Pictorial Supplement* 106 (1974).

Baur, J. I. H., ed. *M. & M. Karolik Collection of American Paintings, 1815–1865*. Cambridge, Mass.: Boston Museum of Fine Arts, 1949.

Brewington, Dorothy E. R., ed. *Marine Paintings and Drawings in Mystic Seaport Museum*. Mystic, Conn.: Mystic Seaport Museum, 1982.

Brewington, M. V., and Dorothy E. R., eds. *Marine Paintings and Drawings in the Peabody Museum*. Salem, Mass.: Peabody Museum, 1968.

Catalog of Paintings. Annapolis, Md.: U. S. Naval Academy Museum, 1954.

Concise Catalogue of Oil Paintings. London: National Maritime Museum, 1988.

A Descriptive Catalog of the Marine Collection at India House. Privately printed at the Sign of the Golden Head, 1935.

Koke, Richard J., comp. *American Landscape and Genre Paintings in the New-York Historical Society: A Catalog of the Collection*. New York: New-York Historical Society and G. K. Hall, Boston, Mass., 1982.

Mariners Museum Catalogue of Marine Prints and Paintings. Boston, 1964.

Old Print Shop. Portfolio (1940–50). New York: H. S. Newman, etc., 1941.

Reilly, Bernard F., ed. *Currier & Ives, A Catalogue Raisonné, 1834–1907*. Detroit: Gale Research Company, 1984.

Schaefer, Rudolph. *J. E. Buttersworth, Nineteenth-Century Marine Painter*. Mystic, Conn.: Mystic Seaport Museum, 1975.

Smith, Philip Chadwick Foster, ed. *More Marine Paintings and Drawings in the Peabody Museum*. Salem, Mass.: Peabody Essex Museum, 1979.

Smithsonian Institution. *National Collection of Fine Arts. Directory to the Bicentennial Inventory of American Paintings Executed before 1914*. New York: Arno Press, 1976, and *Inventory of American Paintings Artists Names*, Washington, D.C., 1984.

EXHIBITION CATALOGUES
American Marine Painting: A Loan Exhibition on Display at Virginia Museum. Richmond: Virginia Museum, 1976.

American Ship Portraits and Marine Paintings. Syracuse, N.Y.: Everson Museum of Art, 1970.

Amerikanische Schiffsbilder Sonderausstellung anlasslich. Hamburg: Altonaer Museum, 1976.

Baur, J. I., comp. *The Coast and the Sea: A Survey of American Marine Painting*. Brooklyn, N.Y.: Brooklyn Museum, 1948.

Brewington, M. V., and Dorothy E. R., eds. *Kendall Whaling Museum Paintings*. Sharon, Mass.: Kendall Whaling Museum, 1965.

Five Centuries of Marine Painting. Detroit: Detroit Institute of Art, 1942.

George Robert Bonfield, Philadelphia Marine Painter, 1805–1898. Philadelphia: Philadelphia Maritime Museum, 1978.

Gerdts, W. H., ed. *Thomas Birch, 1779–1851, Paintings and Drawings*. Philadelphia: Philadelphia Museum, 1966.

Howat, John K., ed. *American Paradise: The World of the Hudson River School*. New York: Metropolitan Museum of Art and Harry N. Abrams, 1987.

Jacobowitz, A., ed. *James Hamilton, 1819–1878*. Brooklyn, N.Y.: Brooklyn Museum, 1966.

James Edward Buttersworth. Mystic, Conn.: Mystic Seaport Museum, 1975.

Olds, Irving Sands. *Catalog of a Special Exhibition of the Irving S. Olds Collection of American Naval Prints and Paintings*. Portland, Maine: Peabody Museum of Salem, 1959.

Pertaining to the Sea. Los Angeles: Los Angeles County Museum of Art, 1976.

Pisano, Ronald G., ed. *Long Island Landscape Painting, 1820–1920*. Boston: Little, Brown, 1985.

Realism and Romanticism in Nineteenth-Century New England Seascape. New York: Whitney Museum of American Art, 1989.

Schweiger, P. D., ed. *Edward Moran, 1829–1901*. Delaware Art Museum, 1979.

Sea and Sail. Portland Museum of Art, 1975.

Workman, Robert G., ed. *The Eden of America: Rhode Island Landscapes, 1820–1920*. Providence, R.I.: Museum of Art, Rhode Island School of Design, 1980.

STUDIES OF INDIVIDUAL ARTISTS
"A. Jacobsen." *Bulletin of the Old Dartmouth Historical Society and Whaling Museum* (1958).

Anderson, Nancy K. *Albert Bierstadt: Art and Enterprise*. New York: Hudson Hills Press in association with the Brooklyn Museum, 1990.

Archibald, Edward H. H. *Dictionary of Sea Painters*. Woodbridge, Suffolk: Antique Collectors' Club, 1989.

Baigell, Matthew. *Thomas Cole*. New York: Watson-Guptil, 1981.

Baker, William Avery. "Elisha Taylor Baker, Marine Painter." *Log of Mystic Seaport* 31, No. 1 (Spring 1979).

Beam, Philip C. *Winslow Homer at Prout's Neck*. Boston: Little, Brown & Co., 1966.

Brewington, Dorothy E. R. *Dictionary of Marine Artists*. Salem, Mass., and Mystic, Conn.: Peabody Essex Museum and Mystic Seaport Museum, 1982.

Brown, Jeffrey R. *Alfred Thomas Bricher, 1837–1908*. Indianapolis: Indianapolis Museum of Art, 1973.

Comstock, H. "Marine Paintings by Two Buttersworths." *Antiques* 75 (1964).

"Dollars and Cents of Art." *Cosmopolitan Art Journal* 4 (1860).

Downes, W. H. "American Painters of the Sea." *American Magazine of Art* 23 (1931).

Driscoll J. P., and Howat, J. K. *John Frederick Kensett*. New York: Worcester Art Museum, 1985.

Ferber, Linda S. *William Trost Richards: American Landscape and Marine Painter, 1833–1905*. Brooklyn, N.Y.: Brooklyn Museum, 1973.

Gaillard, S. "Antonio Jacobsen." *Maine Antiques Digest*.

Halttunen, Lisa. "William Pierce Stubbs, Marine Painter." *Log of Mystic Seaport* 33, No. 3 (Fall 1981).

Havens, G. P. "Frederick J. Waugh, American Marine Painter." *University of Maine Studies* 89 (1969).

Hoffman, K. "The Art of FitzHugh Lane." *Essex Institute Historical Collections* 119 (1983).

Howland, L. "A. Cary Smith." *Nautical Quarterly* 50 (1990).

Jacobsen, Anita. *Frederick Cozzens: Marine Painter*. New York: Alpine Fine Arts, 1982.

Lipman, Jean. *Rediscovery: Jurgan Frederick Huge (1809–1878)*. New York: Archives of American Art, 1973.

Parnes, Stuart. "Frederick S. Cozzens." *Log of Mystic Seaport* 35, No. 2 (Summer 1983).

Peluso, A. J. "The Hoboken School." *Maine Antiques Digest* (1977).

Peluso, A. J. *J. & J. Bard, Picture Painters*. New York: Hudson River Press, 1977.

Peluso, A. J. "Life and Work of Antonio Jacobsen." *Art & Antiques* I (1980).

Weiss, Ila. *Poetic Landscape: The Art and Experience of Sanford R. Gifford*. Newark, Del.: University of Delaware Press, 1987.

Whitmore, Mary. "Antonio Nicolo Gasparo Jacobsen." *American Neptune* 3, No. 3 (July 1943).

Wilmerding, John. *FitzHugh Lane*. New York: Praeger, 1971.

Wilmerding, John. *Robert Salmon, Painter of Ship and Shore*. Salem, Mass.: Peabody Essex Museum of Salem and Boston Public Library, 1971.

SHIP PORTRAITURE
American Neptune Pictorial Supplements

Elliot, Robert S., and McNairn, Alan D., eds. *Reflections of an Era: Portraits of Nineteenth-Century New Brunswick Ships*. Saint John, Canada: New Brunswick Museum, 1987.

Finch, Roger. *The Ship Painters*. Lavenham, Suffolk, England: Terence Dalton, 1975.

Jacobsen, Anita. *From Sail to Steam, the Story of Antonio Jacobsen, Marine Artist: An Artist's Chronicle of the Ships that Sailed the Seas from 1870 to 1920*. Staten Island, N.Y.: Manor Publishing, 1972.

Maloney, Richard C. *Fifty Notable Ship Portraits at Mystic Seaport*. Mystic, Conn.: Marine Historical Association, 1963.

Old Ship Portraits of Kennebunk. Kennebunk, Maine: The Brick Store Museum, 1943.

Poulsen, H. *Danske Skibsportraetmalere*. Copenhagen, 1985.

Schiaffino, P. *The Sailing Ships of Camogli*. Genoa: Gio Bono Ferrari Maritime Museum, 1987.

Smith, Philip Chadwick Foster. *The Artful Roux, Marine Painters of Marseille*. Salem, Mass.:

Peabody Essex Museum, 1978.

Timm, Werner. *Kapitansbilder: Schiffportrats seit 1782*. Bielefeld: Verlag Delius Klasing, 1971.

ART HISTORIES
Berko, Patrick, and Berko, Viviane. *Seascapes of Belgian Painters Born between 1750 and 1875*. Brussels: Editions Laconti, 1984.

Bramsen, H. *Danish Marine Painters*. Copenhagen, 1962.

Brook-Hart, Denys. *British Nineteenth-Century Marine Painting*. Woodbridge, England: Antique Collectors' Club, 1974.

Cordingly, David. *Marine Painting in England, 1700–1900*. New York: Clarkson N. Potter, 1977.

———. *Painters of the Sea. A Survey of Dutch and English Marine Paintings from British Collections*. London: Lund Humphries, 1979.

Gaunt, William. *Marine Painting, An Historical Survey*. New York: Viking Press, 1975.

McLanathan, Richard B. *American Marine Painting*. Boston: Museum of Fine Arts, 1955.

Novak, Barbara J. *American Painting of the Nineteenth Century: Realism, Idealism and the American Experience*. New York: Praeger, 1969.

Richardson, Edgar Preston. *American Romantic Painting*. New York: E. Weyhe, 1944.

———. *Painting in America: The Story of 450 Years*. New York: T. Y. Crowell, 1956.

Wilmerding, John. *American Marine Painting*. New York: Harry N. Abrams, 1987.

CRITICAL STUDIES
Boas, T. S. R. "Shipwreck in English Romantic Painting." *Journal of the Warburg and Courtauld Institutes* 22 (1959).

Dunning, William. *Changing Images of Pictorial Space: A History of Spatial Illusion in Painting*. Syracuse, N.Y.: Syracuse University Press, 1991.

Eager, G. "The Iconography of the Boat in Nineteenth-Century American Painting." *Art Journal* 35 (1976).

Eitner, L. "The Open Window and the Storm-Tossed Boat." *Art Bulletin* 37 (1955).

Fink, L. M., and Taylor, J. C. *Academy: The Academic Tradition in American Art*. Washington, D.C.: National Collection of Fine Arts, 1975.

Flexner, James Thomas. *That Wilder Image: The Painting of America's Native School from Thomas Cole to Winslow Homer*. Boston: Little, Brown, 1962.

Gettens, Rutherford J., and Stout, George L. *Painting Materials: A Short Encyclopedia*. New York: D. Van Nostrand Co., 1942.

Goedde, Lawrence Otto. *Tempest and Shipwreck in Dutch and Flemish Art: Convention, Rhetoric, and Interpretation*. University Park, Pa.: Pennsylvania State University Press, 1989.

Gombrich, Ernest H. *Art and Illusion: A Study in the Psychology of Pictorial Representation*. New York: Pantheon Books, 1965.

Nelson, Harold B. *Sounding the Depths: 150 Years of American Seascape*. New York: American Federation of Arts; San Francisco: Chronicle Books, 1989.

Novak, Barbara. "Basic Aesthetic Guidelines, 1825–1870." *American Art Journal* (Spring 1969).

———. *Nature and Culture: American Landscape and Painters, 1825–1875*. New York: Oxford University Press, 1980.

Parry, Ellwood. *The Art of Thomas Cole: Ambition and Imagination*. Newark, Del.: University of Delaware Press, 1988.

Philbrick, Thomas L. *James Fenimore Cooper and the Development of American Sea Fiction.* Cambridge, Mass.: Harvard University Press, 1961.

Schrier, J. "Art Symbolism and the Unconscious." *Journal of Aesthetics and Art Criticism* 12 (1953).

Stebbins, Theodore E. *The Life and Works of Martin Johnson Heade.* New Haven: Yale University Press, 1975.

Stein, Roger B. *Seascape and the American Imagination.* New York: Clarkson N. Potter, 1975.

Wilmerding, John, ed. *American Light: The Luminist Movement, 1850–1875.* Washington, D.C.: National Gallery of Art, 1980.

Wilton, A. W. "American Light." *Burlington Magazine* 122 (1980).

HISTORY OF PORTS, TRADE, AND SHIPBUILDING
Albion, Robert Greenhalgh. *The Rise of New York Port (1815–1860).* New York: Charles Scribner's Sons, 1939.

———. *Square-Riggers on Schedule: The New York Sailing Packets to England, France, and the Cotton Ports.* Hamden, Conn.: Archon Books, 1938.

Albion, Robert Greenhalgh; Baker, William Avery; and Labaree, Benjamin W. *New England and the Sea.* Middletown, Conn.: Wesleyan University Press, 1972.

Baker, William Avery. *A Maritime History of Bath, Maine, and the Kennebec River Region.* Bath, Maine: Marine Research Society of Bath, 1973.

Bauer, K. Jack. *A Maritime History of the United States.* Columbia, S.C.: University of South Carolina Press, 1988.

Bunting, William Henry. *Portrait of a Port: Boston, 1852–1914.* Cambridge, Mass.: The Belknap Press, 1971.

Johnson, Harry, and Lightfoot, Frederick S. *Maritime New York in Nineteenth-Century Photographs.* New York: Dover Publications, 1980.

Maritime History of New York: A W.P.A. Project. New York: Doubleday, Doran and Co., 1941.

Miller, R. *The New York Coast-Wise Trade, 1865–1915.* Princeton, N.J.: Princeton University Press, 1940.

Morison, Samuel Eliot. *Maritime History of Massachusetts, 1783–1860.* New York: Houghton Mifflin, 1921.

Morrison, John H. *History of New York Ship Yards.* New York: William F. Sametz & Co., 1909.

Rowe, William. *The Maritime History of Maine—Three Centuries of Shipbuilding and Seafaring.* New York: W. W. Norton, 1948.

Tyler, David. B. *Steam Conquers the Atlantic.* New York: D. Appleton-Century, 1939.

HISTORY OF SHIPS
Clark, Arthur H. *The Clipper Ship Era, 1843–1869.* New York: G. P. Putnam's Sons, 1970.

Cutler, Carl. *Greyhounds of the Sea: The Story of the American Clipper Ship.* Annapolis, Md.: U.S. Naval Institute, 1967.

———. *Queens of the Western Ocean: The Story of America's Mail and Passenger Sailing Lines.* Annapolis, Md.: U.S. Naval Institute, 1961.

Dayton, F. E., and Adams, J. W. *Steamboat Days.* New York: Frederick A. Stokes, 1925.

Gibbs, C. R. Vernon. *Passenger Liners of the Western Ocean.* London: Staples Press, 1957.

Hofman, Erik. *The Steam Yachts: An Era of Elegance.* Tuckahoe: John de Graff, 1970.

Howe, Octavius T., and Matthews, Frederick C. *American Clipper Ships, 1833–1858.* 2 vols. Salem, Mass.: Marine Research Society, 1926.

Morrison, John H. *History of American Steam Navigation.* New York: Stephen Daye Press, 1958.

Parker, Capt. H., and Bowen, Frank C. *Mail and Passenger Steamships of the Nineteenth Century.* Philadelphia: J. B. Lippincott.

Ridgely-Nevitt, Cedric. *American Steamships on the Atlantic.* Newark, Del.: University of Delaware Press, 1981.

SHIP DESIGN AND SEAMANSHIP
Bloomster, Edgar L. *Sailing and Small Craft Down the Ages.* Annapolis, Md.: U.S. Naval Institute, 1940.

Bradlee, Francis B. C. *The Ship "Great Republic" and Donald McKay Her Builder.* Salem, Mass.: The Essex Institute, 1927.

Chapelle, Howard Irving. *The Baltimore Clipper: Its Origin and Development.* Salem, Mass.: Marine Research Society, 1930.

———. *The History of American Sailing Ships.* New York: W. W. Norton, 1935.

Fairburn, William Armstrong. *Merchant Sail.* 6 vols. Center Lovell, Maine: Fairburn Marine Educational Foundation, 1945–55.

La Grange, Helen. *Clipper Ships, 1833–1869.* New York: G. P. Putnam's Sons, 1936.

McKay, R. C. *Some Famous Sailing Ships and Their Builder—Donald McKay.* New York: G. P. Putnam's Sons, 1928.

Morris, E. P. *The Fore and Aft Rig in America.* New York: Library Editions, 1927.

Robinson, John, and Dow, George F. *The Sailing Ships of New England.* Salem, Mass.: Marine Research Society, 1924.

Whitter, Bob. *Paddle Wheel Steamers and Their Giant Engines.* Duxbury, Mass.: Steamaster Boats, 1983.

YACHTING
Boswell, C. *The America: The Story of the World's Most Famous Yacht.* New York: David McKay, 1967.

Kelley, James Douglas Jerrold. *American Yachts: Their Clubs and Races.* New York: Charles Scribner's Sons, 1884.

Lawson, Thomas W. *The Lawson History of the America's Cup: A Record of Fifty Years.* Boston: T.W. Lawson, 1902.

Lester, Gary, and Sleeman, Richard. *The America's Cup, 1851–1987: Sailing for Supremacy.* Sydney: Lester-Townsend Publishing, 1986.

Paterson, R. F. *The "America" and the Defenders of the America's Cup, 1851–1930.*

Phillips-Birt, Douglas. *The History of Yachting.* New York: Stein and Day, 1974.

Rayner, Ranulf. *The Winning Moment: Paintings of the America's Cup.* New York: W. W. Norton & Co., 1986.

Rousmaniere, John. *The Golden Pastime, A New History of Yachting.* New York: W. W. Norton & Co., 1986.

Stebbins, Nathaniel Livermore. *Yacht Portraits of the Leading American Yachts, Photographed by N. L. Stebbins.* Boston: Boston Photogravure Co., 1890.

Stephens, William P. *Traditions and Memories of American Yachting.* Camden, Maine: International Marine Publishing Co., 1981.

Thompson, Winfield M.; Stephens, William P.; and Swan, William U. *The Yacht "America."* Boston: Charles E. Lauriat Co., 1925.